Gertrude Stein
1874–1946

Leo Stein
1872–1947

Michael Stein
1865–1938

Sarah Stein
1870–1953

FOUR AMERICANS IN PARIS

THE COLLECTIONS
OF GERTRUDE STEIN
AND HER FAMILY

THE MUSEUM OF MODERN ART, NEW YORK

© Copyright 1970, The Museum of Modern Art
11 West 53 Street, New York, New York 10019
Library of Congress Catalog Card Number: 78-100674
Designed by Carl Laanes
Type set by Boro Typographers, Inc., New York
Printed by Eastern Press, Inc., New Haven, Connecticut
Color plates by Lebanon Valley Offset, Inc., Cleona, Pennsylvania
Bound by Sendor Bindery, Inc., New York

THIS EXHIBITION HAS BEEN MADE POSSIBLE
THROUGH THE GENEROSITY OF
ALCOA FOUNDATION

In its support of the fine arts, Alcoa Foundation seeks to pursue opportunities both to be innovative and to facilitate significant exposure of art to the public. Sponsorship of *Four Americans in Paris* represents innovation in terms of the size of the grant, while amply fulfilling our goal of providing significant exposure of art to many thousands through this catalogue as well as through the exhibition itself. It is an honor to be associated with The Museum of Modern Art, one of the world's premier institutions, in this program. The directors of Alcoa Foundation hope that the pleasure it brings to the public will equal their pleasure in helping to make it possible.

Arthur M. Doty, *President,* Alcoa Foundation

Notes on Contributors

IRENE GORDON, Senior Editor at The Museum of Modern Art, has edited and contributed to numerous Museum publications, notably the *Members Newsletter,* which she edited from its inception in October 1968 to the spring of 1970. The essay published here is part of a larger work on Leo Stein that she has under way.

LUCILE M. GOLSON, who holds a Ph.D. in art history from Harvard University, is Associate Professor of Fine Arts at the University of Southern California in Los Angeles. As a Californian of French descent, she became interested in the Steins as collectors because of this dual heritage and her long association with the San Francisco Museum of Art as researcher and lecturer.

LEON KATZ is professor of Drama at Carnegie-Mellon Institute in Pittsburgh. As an outgrowth of research which he undertook as a graduate student at Columbia University, from which he received a Ph.D. in 1963, he is currently editing for publication the 1901–11 notebooks of Gertrude Stein, which are in the Collection of American Literature, Beinecke Rare Book and Manuscript Library, Yale University.

DOUGLAS COOPER, eminent critic and collector, has written extensively on many aspects of modern art. He is known for his translations of fundamental texts in art history and has directed significant exhibitions of modern masters and movements. He has translated and edited the letters of Juan Gris, has contributed to numerous publications on him, and has participated in many exhibitions of his work.

ELLEN B. HIRSCHLAND holds a degree in Fine Arts from Wheaton College, Norton, Massachusetts. She has worked at The Baltimore Museum of Art and currently teaches adult courses in nineteenth- and twentieth-century art. The article that appears here is part of a larger work Mrs. Hirschland is preparing on her great-aunts Dr. Claribel and Miss Etta Cone.

Contents

FOREWORD
by John B. Hightower

"YOU CAN be a museum or you can be modern, but you can't be both," Gertrude Stein once firmly told one of my predecessors as Director of The Museum of Modern Art. In spite of her dictum, ever since its founding in 1929 this Museum has determined to be both—and perhaps never more so than now, when the needs of a changing society demand of every cultural institution that it reexamine its established patterns and its directions for the future. The Museum has always attempted both to keep abreast of significant current developments in art and to revaluate art of the past—especially the recent past—in the light of history and today's changing standards.

"Four Americans in Paris: The Collections of Gertrude Stein and Her Family" is a unique enterprise for this Museum in several respects. We have presented several exhibitions wholly drawn from individual collections, but the emphasis has been upon the works shown rather than upon the collecting activities or personalities of their owners. This exhibition, however, has a dual aspect. First and foremost, of course, we are displaying works of painting and sculpture of great importance in their own right. At the same time, the exhibition evokes a highly significant moment in the history of art and illuminates the personalities of four members of a noted family, whose daring led them to acquire works by masters of the modern movement before they had attained wide renown. In the process, the Steins became not only the patrons, but also the friends, of some of these artists.

It has been possible to realize this endeavor only because of the effort, cooperation, and dedication of many. Some ninety institutions and individuals, rang-ing geographically from the U.S.S.R. to Australia, and from Norway to Mexico, have generously lent to our exhibition. We are particularly grateful to the many officials of the Soviet Union who have made it possible for two highly important paintings that passed from the hands of the Steins to those of the pioneering Russian collector of modern art, Sergei I. Shchukin, and thence to The Hermitage in Leningrad, to be shown for the first time in America. We express our thanks to Nikolay M. Lunkov, Chief, Cultural Relations Division, Ministry of Foreign Affairs; Mme Yekaterina Furtseva, Minister of Culture, and Vladimir Popov, Deputy Minister; to Mme Maria Feodorovna Edovina, Assistant to the Director, The Hermitage; and in the United States, to the Hon. Anatoly F. Dobrynin, Ambassador of the U.S.S.R. at the Soviet Embassy in Washington. The Hon. Jacob D. Beam, American Ambassador in Moscow, and Edward W. Burgess, Acting Director, Soviet and Eastern European Exchanges Staff, Department of State, Washington, have also lent their good offices in making these loans possible.

Assembling and mounting an exhibition of this magnitude today involves enormous, indeed almost prohibitive, costs. Constantly rising expenses have made it virtually impossible for this Museum and all other cultural institutions to carry on their programs without substantial financial assistance. We are therefore deeply indebted to Alcoa Foundation for the extraordinarily generous grant that has enabled us to present this exhibition. "Four Americans in Paris" is the first major show at The Museum of Modern Art to be underwritten by a single sponsor. The generosity of Alcoa Foundation's gift was matched by an equal enthusiasm on the part of its Directors, both for the concept of the show and for the opportunity of placing on view before large numbers of the American public significant works of art that once belonged to a distinguished American family. In the days when the Steins were forming their collections, the appreciation and patronage of modern art were still restricted to a relatively few venturesome individuals; and the works they assembled were for the private enjoyment of themselves and those who visited their homes. Nowadays, modern art has a wide, enthusiastic audience; and a new type of enlightened patron, the corporation, with a new sense of civic responsibility and a new awareness of this country's cultural needs, is making it possible for ever-increasing numbers of people to enjoy what was formerly accessible only to a few. It is to further these purposes that The Business Committee for the Arts, under the able presidency of Goldwin A. McLellan, has been formed. The gift from Alcoa Foundation points the way to what may be one of the few hopes for the financial salvation of the arts in this country.

As director of the exhibition, Margaret Potter, Associate Curator of Painting and Sculpture, has brought scholarship and imagination to bear on the formidable problem of tracking down the works of art and has used the indefatigable skill of a career diplomat in obtaining the consent of the owners to make them available to us.

Modified versions of "Four Americans in Paris" will be shown in 1971 at The Baltimore Museum of Art and the San Francisco Museum of Art. It is especially appropriate that institutions in these two cities should be participants. The Steins lived in East Oakland, California, from 1880 to 1891—the year of the death of their father, who had been engaged in business in San Francisco. It was in San Francisco that Michael Stein met and married his wife Sarah; it was to northern California that they returned from France in 1935 to spend the last years of their lives; and it is the San Francisco Museum of Art that houses the Sarah and Michael Stein Memorial Collection established in their honor.

It was in Baltimore, where Leo and Gertrude Stein went to live for a time after their father's death, that they met Claribel and Etta Cone. These two sisters became the Steins' lifelong friends, and their own extensive collecting activities were first stimulated by those of the Steins in Paris. The works that the Cones acquired, including many originally owned by the Steins, are now in The Cone Collection of The Baltimore Museum of Art, which plans to publish in its forthcoming *Annual IV* (Spring 1971) selected material from the diaries, letters, and other documents of Dr. Claribel and Miss Etta Cone.

Several articles in this catalogue deal with these relationships. We are grateful to all the contributors to this publication: Irene Gordon, who served as editor as well as author; Lucile M. Golson; Leon Katz; Douglas Cooper; and Ellen B. Hirschland. We believe that their essays, devoted to various aspects of the personalities and collecting activities of members of the gifted Stein family and their circle, will enhance the enjoyment that we hope the exhibition itself may afford those who view it.

INTRODUCTION
by Margaret Potter

IN 1934, Gertrude Stein returned to America for the first time in thirty years. Her first public lecture, in a series which took her to colleges and art clubs throughout the country, was sponsored by The Museum of Modern Art for its members. She spoke about "Pictures," and newspaper accounts report that she succeeded in thoroughly mystifying, and thoroughly charming, her audience.

Two years ago, the Museum had the opportunity to renew its relationship with Gertrude Stein in her capacity as patron and collector of the visual arts. On her death in 1946, Miss Stein had left custody of her cherished collection of paintings to her companion of forty years, Alice B. Toklas. Following the death of Miss Toklas in 1967, these works were about to be sold by Miss Stein's heirs—the children of her nephew Allan, who died in 1951. Under the energetic leadership of Bates Lowry, then the Museum's Director, a plan was formed to enable a group consisting of four of its Trustees—David Rockefeller, Chairman of the Board; John Hay Whitney, a Vice Chairman; William S. Paley, President; and Governor Nelson A. Rockefeller—as well as André Meyer, a Patron of the Museum Collections, to buy this legendary collection. It comprised forty-seven works (thirty-eight by Picasso, nine by Juan Gris), and each member of the group pledged to bequeath at least one of the most important paintings he acquired to The Museum of Modern Art. Seldom has the principle of enlightened self-interest produced so happy a result for all concerned, not the least beneficiary being the Museum itself, whose collection will thus eventually be greatly strengthened by the addition of these major gifts.

It was decided that the paintings from the Gertrude Stein estate should form the nucleus of an exhibition for which the Museum would attempt to reassemble as many as possible of the works of art once owned by Gertrude Stein, her brothers Leo and Michael, and the latter's wife Sarah. The majority of the works exhibited here were acquired in the decade preceding the first World War, when the Steins shared the adventure of collecting modern art in Paris. They have been supplemented by later additions that the Steins made to their respective collections, when they no longer lived in such close association and their tastes tended to diverge.

The process of tracing the ownership of these works has in itself been something of an adventure. Throughout the years, the paintings, sculptures, and prints once owned by the Steins had been dispersed to major public and private collections all over the world. Several outstanding paintings unfortunately were unobtainable for loan, either because of legal restrictions or their physical condition.

We are grateful indeed to the private collectors, museums, and galleries listed on page 154; it is their generosity that has made this exhibition possible. Among so many, it is hard to single out a few; but we are particularly indebted to those who, having previously lent some of these works to the recent Matisse centennial exhibition in Paris, deprived themselves still further for the duration of our show; and to the Trustees of the Göteborgs Konstmuseum and its Director, Karl-Gustaf Hedén, who in spite of the concurrent commemoration of the 350th anniversary of the City of Göteborg agreed to lend their highly important Picasso, *Acrobat's Family with a Monkey.*

Several people have helped in the fascinating detective work of identifying and locating works that left the Steins' possession many years ago. I am particularly indebted to Edward Burns, whose own researches on Gertrude Stein and her family, undertaken for a monograph on the subject, gave our investigations a substantial head start. His generosity in sharing information and his continuing research on our behalf grant him the status of a collaborator on the exhibition. James Mellow, who has been engaged in preparing a book on Gertrude Stein and her circle, also drew willingly on his own archives to aid our search. Several of the contributors to this catalogue, too, made available to the Museum the results of their own extended research. A primary source of information has been old photographs of the two Stein salons in Paris. I am very grateful to Mr. and Mrs. Christopher C. Wright, who lent many otherwise unobtainable photographs for study; and to Donald Gallup, Curator of the Collection of American Literature in the Beinecke Rare Book and Manuscript Library, Yale University, for granting permission to use material from the comprehensive Stein archives there. Special thanks are also due to Daniel-Henry Kahnweiler, Bernheim-Jeune & Cie., and Durand-Ruel & Cie., who kindly facilitated our research by opening their archives. A final word of gratitude must go to Stephen Benedict, whose assistance in matters of diplomacy was indispensable.

Foremost among those within the Museum itself to whom I wish to express particular thanks for his constant interest and support is William S. Lieberman, Director of the Department of Painting and Sculpture. Without his constant cooperation and that of many other colleagues in this and other Departments, neither the exhibition nor its accompanying publication could have been realized.

PICASSO. *Portrait of Leo Stein*. 1906.
The Baltimore Museum of Art, The Cone Collection

A WORLD BEYOND THE WORLD:
THE DISCOVERY OF LEO STEIN
by Irene Gordon

IN PARIS, within the space of a few weeks in the fall of 1905, four Americans bought their first painting by Matisse, discovered the work of Picasso and made their first purchases. The generator of all this activity was a thirty-three-year-old man named Leo Stein. During the next decade he, his sister Gertrude, their brother Michael and sister-in-law Sarah would purchase and propagandize a certain kind of art with such communal vigor that they were thought of as a unit. Clustering them together was only natural; it was the time in their lives when years of intimacy and intellectual exchange had coalesced into a single thrust of energy. Yet they were fundamentally different. As they moved toward the satisfaction of their separate needs, the works of art they had collected with such infectious enthusiasm were gradually dispersed. What brought these four Americans to the adventure that began in the last weeks of October 1905?

"I guess you know my life history well enough," Gertrude Stein wrote a friend who planned to write an article on her, "that I was in Vienna from six months of age to four years, that I was in Paris from 4 years of age to 5, that I was in Cal. from six years of age to seventeen, primary & grammar school East Oakland, Oakwood High School, and that I was born in Allegheny, Penna...."[1]

This outline of Gertrude Stein's earliest years serves as well for her brothers, covering succinctly their birth in Pittsburgh, where their father and one of his brothers had established a clothing business after having severed partnership with other brothers in Baltimore; their childhood years in Europe, where their father deposited the family after the Pittsburgh partnership, too, was dissolved; their return to the United States and final settling in Oakland, where their father forsook the clothing business for street cars, real estate, and the stock exchange. Against this mobile background the adult history of Michael, Leo, and Gertrude Stein begins.

Collections, too, have histories. They begin when a number of random objects are brought together according to a specific view. They go through a period of vigorous growth and eventually reach a point of stasis which is finally resolved by either locking the collection into a permanent whole or dispersing it, making each portion again a random object. Barring acts of God, the entire process is directed by human beings, whose stages of life frequently approximate those of their collections. Gertrude Stein and her family, and the works of art they assembled, were not exempt from this development. The aspect of their lives touched upon here is concerned primarily with the seminal role of Leo Stein, as it is revealed in the correspondence, diaries, photographs, and papers they and their friends have left behind. This documentation does not provide an insight into the interior responses of the Steins, but it does give an idea of the chronological progression that culminated in two of the most revolutionary collections of art ever assembled.

The sequence of events opens with the letter Michael Stein sent from Oakland at the end of January 1891 to his Baltimore relatives informing them of his father's death. He describes the funeral—"attended by many prominent men of San Francisco . . . conducted according to the Jewish rites"—discusses the will, and notes, "The children are all of age except Leo and Gertrude to whom I will act as guardian..."[2] Thus Michael Stein, not quite twenty-six, became head of the family, took charge of its business affairs, and assumed the financial support of his brothers and sisters.

In the early correpondence there is little to be learned about him from his own words, which are generally postscripts to his wife's letters and almost always concerned with business. His care of his youngest brother and sister, even after he ceases being their official guardian, combines an indulgent paternalism with the conscientiousness of the big brother responsible for the money. Never criticizing what they are doing, he keeps them informed of exactly how much money they have, the dates and amounts of each forthcoming installment, and allows them to live free from economic care, with no obligation to defend or explain.

Gertrude's report of their showing him, with great emotion, a photograph of Millet's *Man with a Hoe* and his response that "it is a hell of a hoe,"[3] and Leo's story of his own intense reaction to a painting by Renoir that drew from Michael the observation that the frame wasn't bad,[4] would indicate that although Michael's practicality may have become a family tease, both Leo and Gertrude recognized it as their safety valve. His bantering indifference toward their emotion about art and his scrupulous dedication to accounting for their money should not be misread. His childhood sojourn in Europe had lasted from his ninth to his fourteenth year, during which he was taught French and German, given music lessons, taken to the museums, and exposed to all the things that contribute to an upper-middle-class education. He was a man of taste and intelligence whose inclinations were circumscribed by his sense of duty to the family. "His life is a very hard one these days in many respects," his wife wrote a few years after his father's death, "and he never complains, but it is wearing on him in a way that is no joke, can't even be turned into one by main force."[5]

Michael Stein's wife and sister had diagnosed him as "negatively good." As time passed, however, his wife recognized that the differences in their temperaments made his relations to her "very near heroic . . . nothing I can do for him can approach the sacrifices that he is constantly making for me, that my natural adaptability makes things fun for me that are really torture for him . . ."[6]

The word "vivacious" suits Sarah (Sally) Stein. In her bold round hand she continues conversations she has had with Gertrude about sex and women's problems; writes about plays, concerts, her pregnancy, child rearing; maintains a running report on her victories in the battle of homeopathic versus allopathic medicine; keeps Gertrude informed of the comings and goings, the arguments, engagements, marriages, births, and deaths of scores of relatives and friends. She writes with literary flourishes, sprinkling her pages with "provided I still encumber this earth" and "should I be taken to a better world." She asks Leo to "hunt up" a certain reproduction—"I already see it in a deep grey-green frame, and my head swims."[7] A friend's invitation to come see "the find of the season . . . stirs my blood, and makes visions of coppers and brasses dance before my eyes."[8] Not one to defer to general opinion, she delivers her own views with ardor. The critics' attack on Pinero's *Second Mrs. Tanqueray* on the grounds of impropriety produce an explosion: "And the S.F. papers are going for this play right & left and calling it immoral. Imagine! this *immoral,* and 'Sowing the Wind' *moral,* that sickly sentimental, absolutely irrational dénouement, *moral!* And women, decent women are disgusted with Mrs. Kendal for lending herself to such a part. To my mind, it is the only fine thing she has ever created, the one thing that raises her above the dead level of mediocrity."[9] Sarah's enthusiasms are art, literature, and music. Like Leo, Gertrude, and her husband, she has little in common with the other Stein brother and sister —"Tell Leo that I shall encourage Simon to go East with all my might, for I want him (Leo) to know what it is to be *really* bored to death."[10]

In their exuberance and their desire to shine, Sarah and Gertrude are similar. Their attraction to a central role was expressed early. "I've thought very often of your advice concerning my salon-lady propensities," Sarah wrote after Gertrude had made a visit to San Francisco, "and although occasionally the temptation has been there, I have fought it down, and I can truly say that I am happier."[11] Although in the end it is Gertrude who goes her own way and outlasts Sarah as a "salon-lady," at this point Sarah is the more independent of the two. Especially with regard to Leo.

For the two youngest Steins, Michael and Sarah were the fixed points of family life. But in art and aesthetics, Leo was guide and teacher. He knows the works of art, which are the best books and where to get them, he supplies photogravures, prints, reproductions. His influence extends beyond the visual arts. "I think of Leo very often, these days," Sarah writes from San Francisco when she is taking a literature course. "He certainly did a great deal for me in that first summer of our acquaintance, and when the class marvels at my

Leo Stein
in the courtyard of 27 Rue de Fleurus, Paris. ca. 1906

poetical insight, I grin and charge it up to *his* credit account."[12] She respects him, is undoubtedly in awe of him, but insists upon holding her own—"Leo to the contrary" is frequent in her letters. She was perhaps among the first to discern that Leo's brilliance entailed problems. Following a discussion of one of her own brothers, in whom she sees a conflict of intellect and indolence, she remarks, "In certain respects he is a Leo on a very small scale."[13] Gertrude's spirited disagreement is indicated by Sarah's retreat in her next letter, "As for the Oscar-Leo proposition, I very evidently failed to express myself intelligibly, so will let it drop."[14]

About Gertrude Stein in these early years one surmises rather than learns. The photographs taken on porches, boats, and tennis lawns show a short stocky girl with a friendly face. What comes through about her from her sister-in-law's letters to her, and from the letters and journals of her friends, is what Leo, even after her death, still referred to as "a hearty humanity."[15] In the documents that remain, Leo is the intellectual focus, Gertrude, the social center of their circle of friends. She is in on the visits to the museums, the hunt for Japanese prints, the expeditions the Steins call "junking." There is great talk *from* Leo, but friends talk *with* Gertrude.[16] Her name is connected with their convivial times: "Gertrude and Sister C. came . . . Had a table d'hote dinner at Fiesole and all got drunk";[17] "Gertrude and I lay there and smoked";[18] "Fiesole—a fine walk with Gertrude. Singing in the street in the evening."[19] "Gertrude," Etta Cone said decisively, "is great fun."[20]

Yet there is little evidence of boisterous spirits and good talk in her letters. As is usual with people who live together and have friends in common, Leo and Gertrude frequently wrote joint letters. They write on the same paper and use the same ink, yet the differences are striking. In Leo's sections the ink is dark, the small brisk letters of the words conveying a tension of thought and movement. In Gertrude's portions, loosely looped letters straggle across the page in widely separated lines, the ink a pale tint, as if all of it had floated onto the paper with the most minimum pressure. The baby talk and dialect they both indulge in obviously refer to the jokes of shared experiences. But Leo seems to use them as a release; Gertrude, to create an atmosphere of innocence. She was almost thirty-one years old when, during her second year in Paris, she took "pen in hand" to say "howdy" to Mabel Weeks in New York:

We is doin business too we are selling Jap prints to buy a Cezanne at least we are that is Leo is trying. He don't like it a bit and makes a awful fuss about asking enough money but I guess we'll get the Cezanne. The old master has come back you know our Amico de Sandro which isn't an amico cause its so much better. That is Leo's connoisership. Its a bully picture alright.[21]

The position of intellectual and aesthetic eminence Leo held among family and friends had been allotted to him by Gertrude early in her life. One gathers from their published writings that within the family, he and Gertrude, with only a two-year age difference between them, were always a couple apart—separated by almost a decade from their eldest brother, intellectually and temperamentally unlike their other brother and sister. The two youngest in the family, they were constant companions throughout their childhood and early youth, tramping through the hills munching dried crusts of bread, talking "endlessly about books and people and

The studio at 27 Rue de Fleurus, Paris. ca. 1905

One of the earliest views of the studio showing, among Japanese prints,
two paintings by Gauguin: at left, *Three Tahitians* (Hermitage Museum, Leningrad);
at right, *Sunflowers* (Bührle Collection, Zurich)

things."[22] About a year after their father died, they and their sister Bertha were sent to live with a relative in Baltimore. In the fall of 1892 Leo left for Harvard; the next fall Gertrude enrolled at Radcliffe.

At the end of his third year at Harvard Leo made his first trip abroad as an adult, during which he spent two months in Paris, mostly at the Louvre, and a month in Germany. His observations are interesting not only as the reactions of a bright twenty-three-year-old but for the independence of his responses. He was never to be influenced by accepted standards of quality and greatness, and even at this age he is not swayed by famous names.

I am still as fervent a Rembrandt-ite as ever. For color and composition I swear by Rubens. I haven't grown enthusiastic about any of the Italians except Leonardo. He has here the Mona Lisa and another portrait of a woman also wonderfully subtle. There are some other things by him intrinsically far less interesting. Raphael so far as the Louvre goes is very pretty both in sentiment and execution and Titian I'm not onto yet. Of the early Italians the picture by Giotto is the only one that made much of an impression. . . . In architecture everything, I suppose is more or less disappointing. . . . Cologne cathedral or rather its spires don't come near so close to the mark as they might. In fact they're rather dumpy and the entrance portal is so squeezed between the immense towers that it hasn't any show at all. The flying buttresses and the interior (except in the detail) are fine. Notre-Dame squats, instead of soaring, but its detail is fine. We were out at St. Denis the other day which is thoroughly interesting. The churches here however are generally a nuisance because they never were finished in the style in which they were begun. The first story of the choir may be Romanesque, the upper part early Gothic, with a Late Gothic nave and a Renaissance facade. You can't make head or tail of it and get disgusted with churches and their builders.[23]

While he was still in Europe an uncle offered him a trip around the world, and by December he and his traveling companions were in Kyoto. They lived there for a month, then continued on, to Canton, Ceylon, Egypt. In Cairo he climbed a pyramid, "hardly worth the effort except that it gives you a realizing sense of its size."[24] The trip ended in Europe, where Gertrude joined him, making her first trip abroad since her childhood.

After another year in Cambridge they both returned to Baltimore, took a house together, and entered Johns Hopkins, he studying biology, she, medicine. Gertrude remained there for five years, without finally taking her degree; Leo left after three years. He had already studied history and philosophy and during his college days had spent as much time as he could in the Boston Museum of Fine Arts, the Metropolitan in New York, and the Walters Gallery in Baltimore. Now he decided that he might arrive at the solution of certain aesthetic problems, in which he had long been interested, through the history of art. In October 1900 he settled in Florence to write a book on Mantegna.

Gertrude must have posed the question of their eventually living in New York, for he sent her a lengthy letter considering the problem. In the last decade of his life, after a period of psychoanalysis followed by years of self-analysis, he could describe his early life with diagnostic objectivity. But when he was twenty-eight

Leo, Gertrude, and Michael Stein in the courtyard of 27 Rue de Fleurus, Paris. ca. 1906

he had no such overview; the letter he wrote his sister that first winter in Florence is a self-description filled with humorous, though poignant, insights about himself. He saw as his fundamental problem the fact that there was no one field he was interested in to the exclusion of all others. He complained that he was unteachable and had to examine everything for himself, yet did not have the kind of intellect that could effectively deal with various fields of knowledge. They merely distracted each other, "and in a wild scramble to find answers for the multitudinous problems that arise in my mind I can get nowhere decisively."[25] Among his varied interests, however, some—art, poetry, and aesthetics—were stronger than others and it was desirable that some particular aspects of these should be forced into the foreground. In certain respects it made little difference whether he lived in "a great centre of multitudinous activity like New York" or "a place like Florence where a limited range of activity is almost insisted on," because no matter where he was,

there would be that same . . . quite irresistible tendency to find out one day the truth about the Battle of Vicksburg, another the most recent determination for the date of the second Isaiah, then perhaps Hertwig's answer to Jennings' paper and on a fourth the relation of recalled future time to the possibility of a logically complete induction. All this may seem trivial and I'm the last person to deny that it ought to, while at the same time insisting that as a matter of fact it isn't. . . . I'm all too easily distracted . . . if somebody asks me about the habits of giraffes I'm strongly inclined to look up their anatomy, physiology, and embryology. The amount of time I've wasted because foolish people ask-

ing foolish questions have started my mind off on things it hadn't any business to monkey with . . .

Since he had little hope of controlling his mind, his best recourse was to find restrictive surroundings. Florence, he felt, was a place where he could maintain limits. In the field of Italian art, Mantegna was the only painter who instilled in him a desire to do his best; Leonardo might, but Leo instinctively recognized that he would never come to grips with "that most august theme." In Italy he was safe from the "little Dutchmen," on whom he wanted to do a series of essays, as he also was from Dürer, about whom he wanted to write someday.

He soon found that two other books on Mantegna were already under way, that he was interested in aesthetics and not art history, and that he didn't really want to write the book anyway. But his two winters in Florence were important, he says, for two reasons, ". . . I became really intimate with quattrocento Italian art—the art of Piero della Francesca, Paolo Ucello, Domenico Veneziano, Andrea del Castagno, and the early Siennese—and I discovered pragmatism."[26] But something else about his time in Florence was to have importance in his future. Undoubtedly connected with the knowledge he developed of quattrocento art was his friendship with Bernard Berenson.

In what may be his first letter from Florence, Leo mentions lunching with the Berensons and observes that "he's a good man even if he does think there's no one else in Italy that knows anything about Italian painting, and only one in Germany which the latter B says is an old crank. Unless we should have a rupture, which I don't think very likely, I shall probably see a good deal of them this winter."[27] Although during the next four decades the friendship was to have periods of strain, cordial relations were maintained to the end, perhaps because Leo Stein was willing to overlook what he referred to as "that tremendous excess of the I."[28] "I see a good deal of him," Leo wrote a month after his first letter about Berenson,

i.e., about once a week I go up there, and I find that he distinctly improves. Of course there's that colossal I sticking in him, but it's like a cold bath, after the first plunge you don't mind it. He's thoroughly intelligent in general; as he expressed it, his art studies are the least of his intellectual interests. For metaphysics he doesn't care and he knows little or nothing about physical science, but he is widely and well read in literature, is an enthusiastic Grecian, and rather specially interested in Kulturgeschichte problems of all kinds. . . . [he] has, too, much common sense though his manner tends to disguise this.[29]

His intellectual identification with Berenson was perhaps best expressed when a friend planning a trip to the Low Countries asked Leo to recommend preparatory reading:

As I have indicated to you several times in my gentle and persuasive accents, there will be no good books on art till Berenson and I shall have written them, but if you can't wait until we have finished Italy and undertaken to do Belgium Holland Spain etc., I'll do my best concerning what has hitherto been manufactured.[30]

Even the presence of Berenson, however, could not make up for the limitations he had sought in Florence but found stifling by the end of his second year. He decided to spend the next winter in London; in September 1902 he and Gertrude arrived there, planning to stay five or six months. Despite the fact that Berenson was in England, and through him they met interesting people, Gertrude found London depressing and she soon returned to America. Leo, too, left sooner than he had planned, but for him the time in London was important. It was then that he bought his first oil painting.

He and Gertrude had been buying prints, especially Japanese, for years, and "junking" trips had long been routine. In Florence, Leo had bought intensively, but his acquisitions were still directed toward the minor arts: *Besides books I have gone in for . . . cabinets, tables, chairs, iron boxes, bronze mortars, brass lamps, wooden saints, terra cotta saints, satin hangings, venetian glasses, ivory daggers . . . and finally, to crown this period of wild and venturesome extravagance, a greco roman Dyonysus (where do the y's belong) head in marble . . .*[31] When he bought the oil painting he "felt a bit like a desperado. Oil paintings were for the rich: that was part of the American credo."[32] The picture, by Wilson Steer, did not cost much and as a painting was not important. It was, however, an encouragement: "One could actually own paintings even if one were not a millionaire."[33]

When he left London for Paris in December 1902 he did not intend to remain long. He had been away from America for almost two years and he was getting homesick. While still in Florence he had admitted that though he read the London *Times* every morning, he found it dull when there was no American news in it.[34] And during their short stay in England, he and Gertrude had constant America-vs.-England disputes with Berenson and Bertrand Russell, who could not understand why "in the name of all that's reasonable" the Steins would think of returning to America.

It's quite impossible to persuade them that my Americanism is not a pose but that I really think seriously of returning ... at times it does seem quite impossible. On the whole, however, I remain constant, for after all there is something tonic, even overtonic, about America that I miss here and would not like to miss permanently. If America only were not so far away and if the climate in the possible parts were not so chilly. Those I think are my chief grievances against the land of my birth, though I suppose that they are not very profound ones. Someday I'll make up my mind that I can stand them and then Gertrude and I will retire to Connecticut or Duxbury or somewhere and live happily ever after.[35] Now, via Paris, he was on his way back to America.

But one night in Paris when he was dining with Pablo Casals, as he often did, and expounding on his theories of aesthetics, he suddenly felt himself "growing into an artist." He went back to his hotel, made a fire, took off his clothes, and began to draw from the nude. He spent the next week drawing from statues in the Louvre, then began painting at the Académie Julian. A sculptor cousin recently arrived in Paris had just found a place to live. "As I don't like apartment hunting, I said to him that doubtless he had taken the best he found: what was the next best? He said the next best was 27 Rue de Fleurus. So I settled at 27 Rue de Fleurus."[36]

In his later years Leo Stein dismissed his painting of this time. As with everything else he undertook, he says, it went well at the beginning but then, because he was incapable of building on his skills, it became worse and worse. The single importance he gives to his painting then is that it led him to settle in Paris.

His purchase of the Wilson Steer in London had

Leo Stein
in the courtyard of 27 Rue de Fleurus, Paris. ca. 1905

Leo Stein in the studio at 27 Rue de Fleurus, Paris. ca. 1905

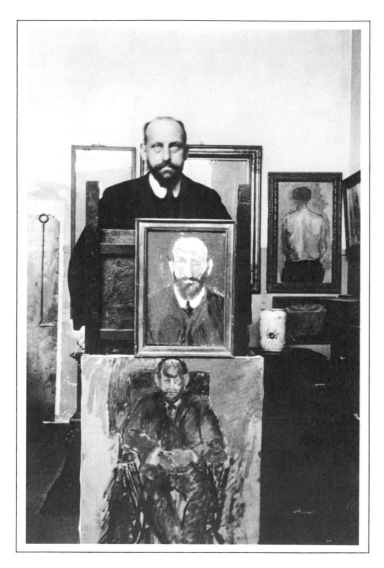

taught him that there were paintings he could afford. In Paris he set out to learn the market. From a dealer who sold him prints some years before he bought a little picture by Du Gardier, "of a woman in white with a white dog on a green lawn."[37] It was an insignificant picture, picked more or less at random and purchased primarily because he spent much time at the dealer's talking about the art scene in Paris, and the sale served as his entrance fee. But the contemporary work he saw did not interest him after first view, and the older paintings were too expensive. Besides, he says, "it was not what I wanted. I wanted an adventure."[38]

Almost a year passed before he bought another painting. In the spring of 1904, Berenson came to Paris and gave Leo advice.

"Do you know Cézanne?" he asked. I said, "No." "Well, look him up." Where?" "At Vollard's on the Rue Lafitte."[39]

Vollard's casual approach to order and his love of conversation put Leo Stein at ease and he went there often. When he had lived in Florence, quattrocento art was being "discovered"; for someone saturated with Piero della Francesca and Domenico Veneziano, he says, Cézanne was easy. Before going to Florence that summer he purchased his first Cézanne, the *Landscape with Spring House* now in the Barnes Foundation.

In Florence he was joined by Gertrude, who had spent the previous months in America.[40] This summer of 1904 Gertrude must have seen her first Cézannes. When Leo told Berenson that he had acted on his suggestion, Berenson informed him there were Cézanne paintings to be seen in Florence. Charles Loeser, a wealthy American living in Florence,[41] had a number of

Michael Stein with portraits of him painted by Leo Stein,
in the studio at 27 Rue de Fleurus, Paris. ca. 1906

Cézannes, which he kept in private rooms apart from the rest of his collection. Leo spent more time that summer with Loeser's Cézannes than with the pictures in the Uffizi, and it would have been totally out of character for Leo not to have shared this latest discovery with his sister.

On returning to Paris after his "Cézanne debauch," he was "a Columbus setting sail for a world beyond the world."[42] In these days of instant awareness of the new, it is interesting to review the position at the beginning of the century of a man who had been studying art for years and now, with the spirit of discovery, was purposively looking for contemporary work in the art center of the world.

He knew Renoir and the other Impressionists from his visits to the Luxembourg and Durand-Ruel and, on the advice of a scholar of Italian Renaissance art, had just learned of Cézanne. He had never heard of Seurat or van Gogh, who had died some twelve years before; nor even of Gauguin, who was given a small memorial exhibition in 1903, the year of his death, at the first Salon d'Automne. He first came to know the work of Toulouse-Lautrec in the special exhibition held at the Salon d'Automne of 1904, and that of van Gogh at the Indépendants special exhibition in the spring of 1905.[43]

Matisse had exhibited two paintings at the 1903 Salon d'Automne, but Leo may have given as little notice to Matisse's work as to Gauguin's. During the first weeks of June 1904, in the very season that Leo had become a habitué of Vollard's and bought his Cézanne, Vollard gave Matisse his first one-man show. Leo's letters of this time are rare, so whether he saw the show and what he thought, if he did, is not clear. Only a few months later, at the 1904 Salon d'Automne, where he "looked again and again at every single picture, just as a botanist might at the flora of an unknown land," he says that Matisse made perhaps the strongest impression on him, "though not the most agreeable."[44]

He bought nothing at this Salon, but in the spring, at the 1905 Indépendants, he bought a Vallotton and a Manguin. In the four months between these exhibitions seven paintings were added to the Wilson Steer, Du Gardier, and the lone Cézanne. They were acquired, according to Leo, in a burst of unanticipated wealth:

My brother, who was our banker, surprised me one day when he said we had eight thousand unexpended francs. As this was regarded as criminal waste, we went at once to Vollard's. . . . I selected two Gauguins, two Cézanne figure compositions, two Renoirs, and Vollard threw in a Maurice Denis, Virgin and Child, *for good measure.*[45]

The letter in which he mentions these new acquisitions is one of the few documents that tell what he was thinking at the time. He explains at the outset that it will be more treatise than letter, for ever since the autumn Salon he has been under the obligation to expound "L'Art Moderne" (which, he is quick to point out, should not be confused with "L'Art Nouveau"). Some ten months before he had not even heard of Cézanne. Now he writes a survey of Impressionist and Post-Impressionist painters in which he not only discusses their individual qualities but touches upon their stylistic origins, what changes they effected in the history of painting, whom they were influencing, and what, in turn, these younger men were doing. Before he reviews the newest developments, however, he discusses "the men of '70 of whom the Big Four and Puvis de Chavannes are the great men and the inspirers in the main of the vital art of today." The Big Four are: Manet—"painter par excellence . . . in sheer power of handling he has perhaps not had his equal in modern times"; Renoir—"the gift of color as no one perhaps since Rubens, except perhaps Fragonard, has had it . . . color handled not as the medium but as the stuff of art"; Degas—"the most distinctively intellectual . . . incomparably the greatest master probably of movement of line, with a colossal feeling for form"; Cézanne—"he has succeeded in rendering mass with a vital intensity that is unparalleled in the whole history of painting. . . . the most robust, the most intense, and in a fine sense, the most ideal of the four." The general drift of his letter was to indicate what he thought of modern art and "to repeat that it vitally goes marching on."[46]

It was probably during the first half of 1905 that he and Gertrude also acquired their Cézanne *Portrait of Mme Cézanne* (Bührle Collection, Zurich)[47] and the *Perseus and Andromeda* by Delacroix (The Baltimore Museum of Art, The Cone Collection), whom Leo considered "by all odds the greatest French painter of his century."[49]

This first act of the Steins' adventure into modern art was not overwhelmingly innovative. It bypassed the accepted art of the time, but it broke no new trails. They were walking on little-traveled ground, but others had already been there. They were among the advanced guard, but they were not pioneers. This remained for the second act.

It began at the Salon d'Automne that opened on October 18, 1905. In notes for a lecture given years later, Claribel Cone recalled the *vernissage:*

Having passed through several of the larger halls we soon found ourselves in a small room . . . which had been set . . . apart for the independent group of which Matisse was chief. . . . We asked ourselves are these things to be taken seriously. As we looked across the room we found our friends earnestly contemplating a canvas— The canvas of a woman with a hat tilted jauntily at an angle on the top of her head—the drawing crude, the colour bizarre.[50]

To Leo Stein, Matisse's *Woman with the Hat* was "a thing brilliant and powerful, but the nastiest smear of paint I had ever seen." After the few days he needed to get accustomed to the way the paint was put on, he bought it.[51] Within weeks of buying his first Matisse he bought his first Picasso.

At the urging of the dealer Clovis Sagot, with whom Leo talked about art and gossiped about scandal, he had come to see at Sagot's an exhibition of a Spanish artist whom Sagot described as "the real thing." When Leo returned a few days later to talk about the Spanish artist named Picasso, whose work he had liked, Sagot had a painting by him, "the picture of a mountebank with wife and child and ape."[52] Leo bought it. Soon after, he learned that a friend knew Picasso, and a few days later he was taken to Picasso's studio in the "Bateau Lavoir." After that meeting he went again to Sagot's, this time with Gertrude. Sagot showed them "a picture of a nude, almost naked little girl with a basket of red flowers. I liked the picture, but Gertrude hated it. A few days later I bought it."[53]

It is unfortunate that just at the moment Leo Stein arrives at the "world beyond the world" he had set out to find, he becomes reticent. All we know of his thoughts during those momentous weeks are the meager sentences he wrote to a friend a few days after the Salon closed:

The Autumn salon is over and has left two pictures stranded in our atelier. All our recent accessions are unfortunately by people you never heard of, so theres no use trying to describe them, except that one of those out of the salon made everybody laugh except a few who got mad about it, and two other pictures are by a young Spaniard named Picasso whom I consider a genius of very considerable magnitude and one of the most notable draughtsmen living.[54]

With the discovery of Matisse and Picasso, the Steins' direction was set. They and their collections entered the period of vigorous growth.

Both Leo and Gertrude as well as the Michael Steins held open house on Saturdays. All kinds of people came: young painters of various nationalities, writers, collectors, dealers, assorted friends, relatives, and acquaintances. Sarah Stein propagandized in her apartment on the Rue Madame; Leo expounded in the studio on the Rue de Fleurus. Leo wrote much in later years about why he abandoned Picasso and stopped buying Matisse, but we do not know what he was saying when he was dedicated to them. "The place," he says, "was charged with the atmosphere of propaganda."[55] The closest we can come to that intensity is the description of such evenings given by Mabel Dodge Luhan:

Leo was always standing up before the canvases, his eyeglasses shining and with an obstinate look on his face that so strongly resembled an old ram. . . . with a fire no one would have suspected in the thoughtful, ramish scholar, he sought in every way to interpret the in-

PICASSO. *"Une tres belle danse barbare"*
(with letter to Leo Stein). Drawing, 1904; letter, ca. 1905.
Collection Mr. and Mrs. Perry Rathbone, Cambridge, Massachusetts

tention in them. . . . *patiently night after night wrestling with the inertia of his guests, expounding, teaching, interpreting . . .*[56]

Many, Mabel Luhan says, went to the Steins "for the fun of it, and half angrily, half jestingly giggled and scoffed after they left."[57] But there were others among them who saw what Leo Stein saw, and their enthusiasm was responsible for carrying the names of Matisse and Picasso outside France.

The collection of Leo and Gertrude Stein was never a collection of specimens; there were many advanced artists of the period who were not represented—Braque, for example, or Vlaminck and Derain. Although from time to time it contained the work of others, the bulk consisted of a Big Four: Renoir, Cézanne, Matisse, and Picasso. The collection Michael and Sarah Stein assembled was devoted predominantly to the work of Matisse.

Leo bought his last Matisse painting in 1908. He bought his last painting from Picasso in 1910, which, he says, he did not really want, but it cleared the account of money he had advanced to him from time to time.[58] As Picasso moved further into Cubism, Gertrude began to buy his work independently. Leo could not accept Cubism as having any permanent value, and his disparagement of Gertrude's writing became more severe as she identified her own aims in literature with those of Picasso in painting. In 1913, Leo and Gertrude separated. They divided their collection, which had been joint property, each choosing the work of the artists that had most meaning for him. Gertrude, who at first had planned to move, remained at the Rue de Fleurus. Leo went to live in Settignano.

The day before he left for Italy, he wrote the coda to

PICASSO. *Leo Stein.* ca. 1905–6.
Collection Mrs. Jerome B. Rocherolle, Stamford, Connecticut

the ten-year adventure into which he had taken his sister, his brother and sister-in-law:

I'm going to Florence a simple minded person of the "Old School" without a single Picasso, hardly any Matisses, only 2 Cézanne paintings & some aquarelles, and 16 Renoirs. Rather an amusing baggage for a leader in the great modern fight. But que voulez vous. The fight is already won & lost. . . . Cezanne & Matisse have permanently interesting qualities, Picasso might have had . . . if he had developed his gifts instead of exploiting those that he did not possess. The general situation of painting here is loathsome with its cubico-futuristic tommyrotting. I don't believe it can last very long, however, as its effectiveness is soon seen through & when no longer curious it becomes a bore. It is, even on the part of the most distinguished representative, nothing better than an exploitation of ingenuity.[59]

In the course of discussing the work of an eminent critic, Leo Stein commented that "when someone who ought to know what he is talking about talks what seems to be nonsense, one tries to find sense in it somehow."[60] Leo Stein presents a similar dilemma. The quality of mind revealed in the wide range of subjects—literature, philosophy, history, politics, psychoanalysis, education, in addition to art and aesthetics—that he discusses in his letters, journals, and essays marks him as a man of supreme intelligence. He notes with some pride that he was the only person anywhere, as far as he knew, who in those early days recognized Picasso *and* Matisse. "Picasso had some admirers, and Matisse had some, but I was alone in recognizing these two as the two important men."[61] Why, then, did he turn away?

His attitude toward Matisse differs from his feeling

PICASSO. *Leo Stein.* ca. 1905–6.
Private collection

about Picasso. Whatever his aesthetic reasons for ceasing to buy Matisse's work—he says the paintings began to be "rhythmically insufficient"[62]—he considered Matisse the only painter of really superior intelligence he had ever known. He was no longer compelled to own Matisse's paintings and was satisfied to see them at exhibitions, but he never lost interest in what Matisse was doing. Matisse, he believed, "always kept moving and generally moved forward."[63] He counted Matisse as a fortunate man who had accomplished his destiny.

Picasso, on the other hand, he saw as a man who had wasted his real gifts on trivialities; had he developed his real genius, Picasso, like Rembrandt or Goya, would have grown to maturity of power. Instead, he set out to rival Cézanne's massive form. But it was just in the area of form, Leo Stein felt, that Picasso's talent was insufficient. In the course of his conflict with Cézanne, his drawing began to lose its nuances. "Its curves grew larger, with marked opposition to straight lines. De-

formation as a means of accent became more and more pronounced. The shapes were simplified and enlarged, but the quality of intrinsic form, in spite of all this, was not achieved."[64] Picasso finally deflected his confrontation with Cézanne by reducing his volumes to formal symbols, which enabled him to exploit his genius for endless ingenuity to the full. Cubism, Leo Stein believed, was an art of invention rather than expression and thus staled rapidly. In his view, it was only Picasso's genius for devising new combinations that kept Cubism fresh, and it was his infinite inventiveness that constituted the main lines of the history of Cubism.

With his refusal to accept Cubism as a valid art form, Leo Stein became a "rank outsider . . . no longer a prophet in Israel . . . at best only a Jeremiah."[65] He was, he said, a cheerful one and took his deposition good-humoredly. But with Leo's departure, the period of vigorous growth of the collections of Gertrude Stein and her family ended.

Notes

I should like to thank Donald Gallup, Curator of the Collection of American Literature, and the staff of the Beinecke Rare Book and Manuscript Library, Yale University, for the extraordinary generosity with which they make their holdings available for study. Charles Parkhurst and Mary Dickerman of The Baltimore Museum of Art have been equally generous with the material in the Cone Archives and have responded with good humor to innumerable requests.

The date of a letter without additional notation indicates that it was inscribed by the writer of the letter. A year in brackets indicates that it has been ascribed by either Yale University Library or the author on the basis of external evidence. All quotations have been transcribed verbatim.

1   Gertrude Stein to Harriet Lane Levy, undated letter [1914?], Collection of American Literature, Beinecke Rare Book and Manuscript Library, Yale University (hereafter given as "Yale").
2   Michael Stein to Meyer Stein, letter of January 28, 1891 (Yale). The children of Daniel (1832-1891) and Amelia Keyser Stein (1842-1888) were: Michael, born 1865; Simon, born 1868; Bertha, born 1870; Leo, born 1872; and Gertrude, born 1874.
3   *Lectures in America,* New York: Random House, 1935, p. 65.
4   *Journey into the Self: Being the Letters, Papers & Journals of Leo Stein,* ed. by Edmund Fuller, New York: Crown Publishers, 1950, p. 19.
5   Sarah Stein to Gertrude Stein, letter of October 29 [1894] (Yale).
6   *Ibid.*
7   Sarah Stein to Leo Stein, letter of November 16, 1896 (Yale).
8   Sarah Stein to Gertrude Stein, letter of September 19, 1898 (Yale).
9   *Ibid.,* letter of October 29 [1894] (Yale).
10 *Ibid.,* letter of December 8 [1896] (Yale).
11 *Ibid.,* letter of October 30 [1899] (Yale).
12 *Ibid.*
13 *Ibid.,* letter of September 22 [1895] (Yale).
14 *Ibid.,* letter of October 8, 1895 (Yale).
15 Leo Stein to Hiram Haydn, letter of July 21, 1947 (Yale).
16 These prepositions are used, seemingly unconsciously, by Etta Cone in her travel journal of 1901, now in the Cone Archives, The Baltimore Museum of Art (hereafter given as "Baltimore").
17 Etta Cone's travel diary of 1903 (Baltimore).
18 *Ibid.*
19 Diary of Mabel Foote Weeks, entry of July 15, 1905 (courtesy of Mr. and Mrs. Christopher Wright, New York). Miss Weeks, for many years a member of the faculty and administrative staff of Barnard College, first met Leo and Gertrude about 1893 or '94 when she was a student at Radcliffe. She and Leo maintained an active correspondence throughout his life.
20 Etta Cone's travel diary of 1903 (Baltimore).
21 Gertrude Stein to Mabel Foote Weeks, undated letter [December 1904?] (Yale).
22 Leo Stein, *Journey into the Self,* p. 185.
23 Leo Stein to Gertrude Stein, letter of July 30, 1895 (Yale). Leo Stein tended to fit his clauses to the width of the page he was writing on and frequently did not use commas because the edges of the paper served as pauses. Since these boundaries are lost when the letters are transcribed, commas have been inserted occasionally in the interests of clarity.
24 Leo Stein to Gertrude Stein, letter of March 13, 1896 (Yale).
25 *Ibid.,* letter of December 20, 1900 (Yale).
26 *Appreciation: Painting, Poetry and Prose,* New York: Crown Publishers, 1947, p. 147.
27 Leo Stein to Mabel Foote Weeks, letter of October 9, 1900 (Yale).
28 Leo Stein to Gertrude Stein, letter of October 11, 1900 (Yale).
29 Leo Stein to Mabel Foote Weeks, letter of November 7 [1900] (Yale).
30 *Ibid.,* letter of December 2, 1900 (Yale).
31 *Ibid.,* letter of December 20, 1901 (Yale). Almost all the items mentioned became part of the furnishings of the Paris apartment he and Gertrude shared and can be seen in the photographs of the studio taken over the years.
32 *Appreciation,* p. 150.
33 *Ibid.*

34 Leo Stein to Mabel Foote Weeks, letter of March 15, 1902 (Yale).

35 *Ibid.*, letter of September 19, 1902 (Yale).

36 *Appreciation,* p. 152.

37 *Ibid.*, p. 154.

38 *Ibid.*

39 *Journey into the Self,* p. 204.

40 Gertrude had moved in with Leo in the fall of 1903, but, according to Leo, she agreed to stay only on the condition that she would make an annual visit to America: "I said she'd probably get used to it, but Gertrude is naturally dogmatic and she said no, she was like that, and that was like her, and so it must be. That year she went to America for a visit and thirty-one years later she went again. No one really knows what is essential" (*ibid.*, p. 320).

Gertrude's first return visit to America took place in the spring of 1904: in a letter written in Boston, February 15, 1904 (Yale), Emma Lootz Erving wishes Gertrude "Bon voyage" and asks her to plan to spend the week beginning April 11 with her; letters dated May 30, June 21, and June 24, 1904, from Claribel Cone to her sister Etta (owned by Ellen B. Hirschland) indicate that Gertrude sailed back to Europe with Etta Cone in early June 1904.

41 Described by Leo as "the son of Brooklyn's Macy's" (*Appreciation,* p. 155).

42 *Ibid.*, p. 157.

43 Leo Stein (*ibid.*) locates the van Gogh exhibition at the Salon d'Automne of 1904; however, the special exhibitions at that Salon were of the work of Cézanne, Puvis de Chavannes, Redon, Renoir, and Toulouse-Lautrec. The special exhibition of van Gogh's work was held the following spring at the Indépendants. This is one of the rare times that Leo Stein's memory is faulty; the accuracy with which his recollections agree with the documents of the time is remarkable.

44 *Ibid.*

45 *Ibid.*, pp. 194–95. On the basis of photographs of the Rue de Fleurus studio, these paintings may be identified as: Gauguin, *Sunflowers* (Bührle Collection, Zurich) and *Three Tahitians* (Hermitage, Leningrad); Cézanne, *Bathers* (Barnes Foundation, Merion, Pa.) and *Bathers* (Plate 20); Renoir, *Brunette* (Plate 22) and *Two Nudes* (Barnes Foundation); and Maurice Denis, *Maternité* (*Mother in Black*) (Collection D. Denis, St.-Germain-en-Laye). Par value of 8,000 francs was approximately $1,500 in 1904, which would average out to about $250 for each of the six paintings.

The acquisition of the paintings within these four months is implied in an undated letter to Mabel Foote Weeks (Yale) in which Leo mentions the special Toulouse-Lautrec exhibition at the recent Salon d'Automne, placing the letter after November 1904, but does not include in the list of painters whose works they have bought—Renoir, Cézanne, Gauguin, Maurice Denis—the names of Vallotton and Manguin, putting it before the Indépendants, which opened in late March 1905.

However, if we assume that two letters at Yale are a response to Gertrude's enthusiastic report of the windfall, the acquisition narrows down to November 1904. In a letter to Gertrude of November 20, 1904, Emma Lootz Erving, writing from Washington, D.C., joshes, "You people . . . with all your surplus money. . . . I repeat that it ain't good taste to flaunt your wealth in the eyes of paupers . . ."; and in her next letter (December 13, 1904) continues to jest, "I think you would be ashamed to flaunt your purchases before my poverty stricken face. . . . You must have some dandy things. Why don't we see some Renoirs and Cezannes over here?"

46 Leo Stein to Mabel Foote Weeks, undated letter [early 1905?] (Yale).

47 Perhaps the Cézanne painting for which they were selling Japanese prints, mentioned in Gertrude Stein's undated letter to Mabel Foote Weeks quoted above.

48 The Delacroix is mentioned in a letter of September 2, 1905, written to Gertrude by Emma Lootz Erving (Yale), who visited the studio while the Steins were in Italy.

49 *Appreciation,* p. 198.

50 Among papers owned by Ellen B. Hirschland. The friends referred to here seem to be Michael and Sarah Stein, who by then were also living in Paris.

51 *Appreciation,* p. 158. Years later Sarah Stein said that she and Leo both decided that the painting should be acquired by the family; see Fiske Kimball, "Matisse: Recognition, Patronage, Collecting," *Philadelphia Museum Bulletin,* March 1948, p. 37.

52 *Appreciation*, p. 169. The painting referred to is now known as *The Acrobat's Family with a Monkey* (Plate 40).

53 *Ibid.*, p. 173. The painting referred to is *Young Girl with a Basket of Flowers* (Plate 32).

Leo's account makes it seem as though these events occurred over an extended period some time after the purchase of the Matisse. However, in the expense book kept by Etta Cone, who was then living in Paris, there is an entry of November 2, 1905, noting a payment of 120 francs for "1 picture 1 etching Picasso" (Baltimore). If this purchase took place in Picasso's studio, to which Etta Cone was taken by the Steins, it would mean that the discovery, purchases, meeting, and subsequent visits all occurred within two weeks, that is, between the first days of the autumn Salon, which opened on October 18 in 1905, and November 2, the date of Etta Cone's entry. If the November 2 entry merely records a purchase Etta Cone made at Sagot's, it indicates how quick Leo was to communicate his discoveries and influence his friends.

54 Leo Stein to Mabel Foote Weeks, letter of November 29, 1905 (Yale). This restraint, however, seems not to have been arbitrary; almost twenty years later, in his review of an exhibition, he refrains from speaking of particular painters or pictures, "for nothing seems to me more futile than talk of works that have not been seen" ("A New Salon in Paris," *New Republic*, July 30, 1924, p. 271).

55 *Appreciation*, p. 58.

56 *Intimate Memories, 2: European Experiences*, New York: Harcourt, Brace, 1935, pp. 321–22.

57 *Ibid.*, p. 322.

58 *Appreciation*, p. 187. He does not name this painting but identifies the Matisse (*ibid.*, p. 162) as *The Blue Nude* (Plate 17).

59 Leo Stein to Mabel Foote Weeks, letter of April 2, 1914 (Yale).

60 *Appreciation*, p. 206.

61 *Ibid.*, p. 188.

62 *Ibid.*, p. 166.

63 *Ibid.*

64 "Pablo Picasso," *New Republic*, April 23, 1924, p. 230.

65 Leo Stein to Mabel Foote Weeks, letter of February 4, 1913 (Yale).

MATISSE. *Portrait of Michael Stein.* 1916.
San Francisco Museum of Art,
gift of Nathan Cummings
to the Sarah and Michael Stein Memorial Collection

MATISSE. *Portrait of Sarah Stein.* 1916.
San Francisco Museum of Art,
gift of Mr. and Mrs. Walter A. Haas
to the Sarah and Michael Stein Memorial Collection

THE MICHAEL STEINS OF SAN FRANCISCO: ART PATRONS AND COLLECTORS

by Lucile M. Golson

"SHE KNOWS more about my paintings than I do,"[1] Henri Matisse is said to have remarked about Sarah Samuels Stein in a unique testimonial of a great artist to his patron and friend. During the year of the Matisse centennial, and on the occasion of the exhibition of the collections of the Stein family, it seems appropriate to recall the exceptional contribution made to the understanding and encouragement of Matisse's art by this San Francisco family, and especially by Sarah and her husband, Michael Stein.[2] The roles and personalities of these two early and faithful supporters of Matisse have been somewhat overshadowed by the flamboyance of Michael's famous sister Gertrude and gifted brother Leo. Matisse himself, however, in his refutation of Gertrude Stein's *Autobiography of Alice B. Toklas,* declared that "Madame Michel Stein, whom Gertrude Stein neglects to mention, was the really intelligently sensitive member of the family. Leo Stein thought very highly of her because she possessed a sensibility which awakened the same thing in himself."[3]

What prepared the Steins to become such active patrons of modern art during the decisive years preceding the first World War is a matter for speculation. With roots in the eastern United States—Pittsburgh and Baltimore—and further back in Germany, the Stein brothers and sisters had their first cultural experiences as children in Europe—in Vienna and, for a year, in Paris. By 1880, the family settled in East Oakland, California. Gertrude has described the life there as happy,[4] despite a demanding, erratic father and an ailing though loving mother. According to Alice B. Toklas,[5] the Stein children were not particularly oriented by their parents toward the arts or literature, though Gertrude in *The*

Autobiography of Alice B. Toklas maintains that she absorbed Shakespeare in her eighth year, and Leo mentions that his interest in pictures began early, that he was always trying to draw, and that he clipped woodcuts out of magazines and mounted them;[7] he also recalls that when he was fourteen his brother Michael, who had been at college in the East, brought back etchings.[8]

Opportunities to see and experience art were not lacking in northern California at this time. Although, compared to eastern seaboard cities, Oakland and San Francisco might be considered as offering little to prospective art lovers, collecting activities were extensive and collectors generous in lending for public exhibitions. Among the events of their girlhood days in the 1880s, both Gertrude Stein and Alice B. Toklas recalled being taken to see Millet's *Man with a Hoe*.[9] The most famous work in the William H. Crocker Collection, this painting, according to family tradition, had been acquired in Paris by the owner himself.[10] It was the first important work in a collection that by the early 1890s would include paintings by artists ranging all the way from Delacroix and Courbet to Degas and Pissarro, and even a *Poplars* and one of the Haystack series by Monet.[11] These were shown in several exhibitions during the 1890s.[12]

Public art activity in San Francisco had centered around the Mercantile Library Museum Room until the San Francisco Art Association, founded on March 28, 1871, began to exhibit in the Mark Hopkins mansion on Nob Hill.[13] In the 1880s, the University of California at Berkeley already prided itself on a budding collection of American paintings and old masters (most of them copies).[14] The first public art museum in San

Sarah, Allan, and Gertrude Stein.
San Francisco, summer 1899

Francisco was founded in 1895. It had its origin the year before, when the Fine Arts Building of the Midwinter International Exposition was turned over to the show's chief organizer, the publisher M. H. De Young, for the purpose of establishing a permanent art collection for the city. At that time the museum, located in the Golden Gate Park, was called simply the Memorial Museum, but in 1921 it took the name of its founder and became the M. H. De Young Memorial Museum.[15]

San Franciscans were especially interested in Oriental art, and Chinese bronzes and Japanese prints were prized. As a young couple, Michael and Sarah Stein surrounded themselves with Oriental objects and furniture. These figure conspicuously in old photographs owned by the family, and some were taken with them to Paris for their Rue Madame apartment.

Born in Pittsburgh on March 26, 1865, Michael D. Stein had returned East to attend college; after studying at Johns Hopkins University, he joined his father in the management of one of San Francisco's street railways. When, following his mother's death in 1888, his father died in 1891, Michael—two months shy of twenty-six—succeeded him as family head and also became assistant superintendent of the Omnibus Cable Company, of which his father had been vice-president. In 1893, in the first business coup of his career, Michael Stein successfully promoted the consolidation of the street railways and the following year became second vice-president of the combined system, the Market Street Railway Company, of which he became division superintendent in 1895.[16] Several stories have been told about Michael's aversion to the business world and his sympathy for the working man, which led him to side

Leo, Gertrude, and Allan Stein, unidentified woman, Sarah and Michael Stein
in the courtyard of 27 Rue de Fleurus, Paris. ca. 1905

with the unions during the cable-car strike of 1902.[17] These inclinations no doubt led to his premature retirement in about 1903 and his decision to seek in Europe a more congenial and leisurely life.

A gentle and reticent man, ever helpful to his friends, Mike, as he was known, was to remain the figure of the solicitous, reasonable elder brother to Leo and Gertrude. According to Alice B. Toklas, he was "a really lovely person, a beautiful character and Gertrude was devoted to him."[18] His interests at first centered on music and the theater. The surprisingly few references to Michael in the published letters of Gertrude and Leo tend to give the impression that his role in relation to art involved exclusively the practical aspects of buying and installing.[19] In actuality, however, although he was apt to rely on his wife's judgment in art, Michael was far from being merely a passive spectator. Annette Rosenshine, who lived with the Steins in Paris from 1906 to 1908, describes his pleasure at showing American visitors around the museums and galleries. He even took her one day to the Hôtel Drouot, where he purchased a fine little Cézanne, *Portrait of the Artist's Son, Paul* (Mr. and Mrs. Henry Pearlman Collection, New York), for which he paid the equivalent of $200—a then-incredible sum; the next day, a Paris newspaper labeled him the "crazy American."[20]

Michael Stein's marriage to the vivacious Sarah Samuels in 1893 suited his retiring nature.[21] Born in San Francisco on July 26, 1870, Sarah—or Sally, as she was known—was the second child of a prominent family. A bright young girl who graduated from high school at the age of fifteen as class valedictorian, she is said to have studied painting before her marriage.[22] Appraisals of her personality have varied considerably. Annette Rosenshine gives this description of her as she was after having lived in Paris for a few years: "Her appearance suggested comfort, a good San Francisco bourgeoise, not a vestige of modishness, of Parisian chic."[23] Portraits painted later, notably by Matisse, reproduce sensitive and intelligent features. Others have stressed an emotional, affectionate nature, marked by enthusiasm and singleness of purpose, and not without a degree of intolerance. Matisse was her great man; according to Harriet Lane Levy, Sarah's eloquence "mesmerized" others into accepting him as *the* painter of his generation. Sarah's early letters to Gertrude Stein reveal a warm, protective attitude toward her younger sister-in-law. But their relations soon are less clear. Some rivalry in matters of art may have existed, together with a feeling of insecurity on the part of Sarah, as tastes diverged and Gertrude developed into a rising author.

Late in 1903, the Michael Steins and their eight-year-old son Allan settled at 58 Rue Madame, in a quiet section of the Left Bank, close to Leo and Gertrude who had preceded them to Paris shortly before and were living in the Rue de Fleurus. The Rue Madame apartment was a converted loft (rather curiously, in a former Protestant church building), with a potbellied cast-iron stove in the large living-dining room. Photographs of this room show it filled with Italian furniture that the Steins collected with a passion, together with Persian rugs and Oriental objects brought from San Francisco. A dazzling array of their rapidly growing collection of modern paintings was ranged along the walls. For a while, works by Cézanne, Renoir, and even Picasso, such as the sensitive portrait of Allan painted in 1906 (page

Reading clockwise: Leo, Michael, Allan, Sarah, and Gertrude Stein
with unidentified woman and boy. Villa Bardi, Fiesole, summer 1905

83), held their own among those by Matisse, but soon the number of the latter became overwhelming.[24]

The large room with its fine paintings was the setting for a weekly open house on Saturday evenings at nine. According to Ambroise Vollard, the Steins were "the most hospitable people in the world."[25] Americans were quite a novelty in Paris, and the two Stein salons with their display of avant-garde art became the fashionable places to visit for connoisseurs and dilettantes alike. These were not merely social occasions:

Beautifully gowned in original costumes, antique jewelry . . . Sarah sat on the couch in the corner explaining to everybody the greatness of Matisse. People listened to her, unconvinced, but overwhelmed by her enthusiasm and authority.[26]

Serious philosophical discussions are said to have taken place at the Michael Steins' salon, where Matisse reportedly met for this purpose with such aestheticians and scholars as Matthew S. Prichard and Georges Duthuit.[27] Among the illustrious visitors who availed themselves of the almost unlimited hospitality of the Steins were the famous Russian collector Sergei Shchukin, the Cone sisters of Baltimore (who greatly profited by the experience and eventually went on to outdo the Steins in their collecting zeal), and on a rare occasion even Dr. Albert Barnes of Pennsylvania.[28]

Although comfortable, the Steins were not affluent. They have been described as leading a rather frugal life in Paris, denying themselves the pleasure of attending a play or a concert in order to be able to travel and to concentrate on their all-consuming passion for art.[29] But in those early years, they never spent more than a few hundred dollars on the masterpieces of their choice.[30]

Sarah Stein's relation to Matisse was more than that of a propagandizer and collector of his work. Following the Salon d'Automne of 1905, after Leo Stein had taken his brother and sister-in-law to meet the artist in his studio, a close friendship developed between the Michael Steins and the Matisses, and the two families visited back and forth.[31] The painter seems to have found in Sarah a confidante, even a critic whose judgment he valued. According to Therese Jelenko, Matisse would come regularly to the Rue Madame, carrying bundles of his pictures, and Sarah "would tell him what she thought of things, sometimes rather bluntly. He'd seem to always listen and always argue about it."[32] Annette Rosenshine adds:

I recall seeing Matisse in the Steins' apartment when he was in the throes of struggling with a new creative expression. There he found solace in unburdening his latest problems and uncertainties to Sarah Stein, knowing that he would receive sensitive, sympathetic understanding. The talk and friendship were of value to him. In later years, after the Steins' return to America, he corresponded with Sarah, telling her of his work and over the years his loyalty to her never flagged.[33]

In the winter of 1907/8 Sarah Stein, who was receiving informal instruction in painting from Matisse, was instrumental in helping him to organize a short-lived art academy. A perceptive as well as an attentive listener, she took notes of her teacher's comments, which are among the most remarkable statements of an artist's philosophy and views on art.[34]

The gathering of a great collection is in itself a work of art. Michael and Sarah Stein, by their almost exclusive concentration on the work of Matisse, demon-

Michael and Sarah Stein, Henri Matisse, Allan Stein, and Hans Purrmann
in the apartment of Michael and Sarah Stein, 58 Rue Madame, Paris. Late 1907

On wall at left: MANGUIN *La Coiffure* (Private collection, Lausanne); PICASSO *Seated Woman with a Fichu* (Private Collection, Detroit)

First file, top to bottom: MATISSE *Pink Onions* (Statens Museum, Copenhagen); MATISSE *Male Nude* (Private collection, San Francisco)

Second file: MATISSE Unidentified painting; MATISSE *Woman and Still Life* (Private collection, San Francisco); MATISSE *Reclining Nude, I* (Private collection, Cal.); MATISSE *Nude Before a Screen* (Collection Robert Ardrey and Helen Johnson Ardrey, Norman, Okla.)

Third file: MATISSE *Olive Trees* (Private collection, Copenhagen); MATISSE *Study for Joy of Life* (Collection Mr. and Mrs. Walter A. Haas, San Francisco); MATISSE *Portrait of Mme Matisse* ("The Green Line") (Statens Museum, Copenhagen)

strated a prophetic gift for uncovering masterpieces at their inception, and in the process they succeeded in capturing something of the artist's personality. Many of their choices appear even more revealing in the light of Matisse's own eloquent statements. Particularly noteworthy is the importance given to the human face and figure, reflecting the painter's own feelings: "It is through it [the human figure] that I best succeed in expressing the nearly religious feeling that I have towards life."[35]

The Steins' greatest activity was concentrated in the few years between 1905 and 1908. But two periods and two collections are involved. The first and more important collection was largely sold away after the first World War, following the Steins' recovery of most of the nineteen paintings which they had lent to a large Matisse retrospective on view at the Gurlitt Gallery in Berlin when hostilities broke out in August 1914, and which had been confiscated as alien property when the United States entered the war in 1917.[36] After the war, the Steins continued to collect but on a reduced scale; and when they left France in 1935 to return to Palo Alto, California, their collecting activities had been virtually at an end for some years.

Every phase of Matisse's early development was represented, starting with *The Open Door* of 1896 (now in a private collection), painted when the artist was quite close to the *intimisme* of his contemporaries the Nabis. In its simplicity and poetry of light, this picture also evokes the art of such seventeenth-century Dutch interior painters as Pieter de Hooch. The *Sideboard and Table*, 1899 (Plate 3) already exemplifies Matisse's "pre-fauve," pointillist technique, a shimmer of warm tones over an intricate spatial arrangement. Quite different in its austere color is the forceful, Cézannesque *Woman with Black Hair* of about 1902 (Mrs. Andrew Cole Collection, San Francisco).

One of Matisse's key pictures, the *Joy of Life*, 1905–6 (Barnes Foundation, Merion, Pennsylvania) was bought by Leo; but the Michael Steins revealed a penetrating and sympathetic interest for the creative process that engendered it by acquiring several important studies for this painting: the *Landscape at Collioure*, 1905 (Statens Museum for Kunst, Copenhagen), and the *Study for Joy of Life*, 1905 (Mr. and Mrs. Walter A. Haas Collection, San Francisco), always one of Sarah Stein's favorites. These enable the viewer to follow the slow and thoughtful maturation involved in the creation of the *Joy of Life*, even if the artist's intent in the paintings was primarily to "render the emotion they awaken"—a statement Matisse made concerning his still lifes that might equally well apply to most of his pictures.

These extensive acquisitions followed the first bold venture involving the four members of the Stein family, the purchase of the *Woman with the Hat* (Mr. and Mrs. Walter A. Haas Collection, San Francisco), which was the big sensation of the 1905 Salon d'Automne and was one of the works chiefly responsible for the label of "fauves" jocularly applied by the critic Vauxcelles to Matisse and his group in response to their paintings in that show. Therese Jelenko, who accompanied the Steins on their visits to the Salon, recalls: "I still can see Frenchmen doubled up with laughter before it, and Sarah saying 'it's superb' and Mike couldn't tear himself away."[37] Traditional in subject matter and costume, it remains one of Matisse's most significant and revolutionary statements. The transposition of nature for the sake of expression and the importance of color in achieving that aim appear fully for the first time in the *Woman with the Hat*, with its richly contrasted palette and its modeling through complementaries rather than tonal values. The story goes that the model, Mme Matisse, was dressed all in black and seated against a white wall. The painting remained in the Rue de Fleurus apartment, the last Matisse owned by Gertrude, who sold it to Michael in 1915.[38] It was one of the few works that Sarah and Michael Stein kept over the years and took back with them to California.

In 1906, Michael and Sarah, on their own this time, bought the even bolder *Mme Matisse ("The Green Line")* of 1905 (Statens Museum for Kunst, Copenhagen). It too is a portrait of the artist's wife, but a different technique of flat pigments applied in a heavy impasto to create strongly delineated forms produces a powerfully expressive contrast of arbitrary colors. Striking are the warmth and seriousness of expression, that quality ever present in portraits by Matisse of the "deep gravity which persists in every human being." This work, the equally bold little *Nude before a Screen* (Plate 15), and a third, unidentified painting were taken by the Steins to San Francisco when they returned there for a few months after the 1906 earthquake and fire. They were the first works by Matisse to be seen in America, and the shocked reactions of her friends back home were humorously reported by Sarah Stein in a letter to Gertrude.[39] But a New York friend, the painter George F. Of, was so impressed by the paintings that he entrusted Sarah with securing a Matisse for himself. She chose *Nude in a Wood*, ca. 1905 (now in the Brooklyn Museum), which became the first work by Matisse

to be acquired by a collector in the United States. The Michael Steins further continued their efforts to make Matisse better known in this country by lending two of their best paintings by him to the Armory Show in New York in 1913.[40]

The year 1906 marked the high point of the Steins' collecting activity; they also acquired the *Young Sailor, I* (Private collection, Norway) and *The Gypsy*, 1906 (Musée de l'Annonciade, St.-Tropez). The latter is related to the *Nude before a Screen* by its color contrast and distorted, simplified forms, almost expressionistic in intensity. An amazingly direct *Self-Portrait*, 1906 (Statens Museum for Kunst, Copenhagen), which Gertrude Stein thought too intimate to be shown publicly, introduces Matisse's development toward a more structured, restrained style and the search for essentials—a development represented also in the Steins' collection by *The Hairdresser* of 1907 (Staatsgalerie, Stuttgart). An increased use of rhythmic, constructive lines is apparent in this painting. "I try to condense the meaning of this body of a woman by drawing its essential lines" in order to achieve "a wider meaning, a more comprehensively human one," Matisse was to write the next year.

In contrast to these stunning, often large works, a number of fresh landscapes, such as the two seascapes of 1905 (San Francisco Museum of Art, Mildred B. Bliss Bequest) indicates Matisse's continuing links with Neo-Impressionism. A few, but significant, still lifes complete the Steins' selection at this time. They range from the low-keyed *Study in Blue*, 1903 (Brayton Wilbur Collection, Burlingame, California), evocative of both Chardin and Cézanne, to the deceptively simple and gaily patterned *Pink Onions*, 1906 (Statens

Museum for Kunst, Copenhagen), suggestive of Near Eastern influences. The *Interior with Eggplants* of 1911 (Musée de Peinture et de Sculpture, Grenoble) is the most impressive of the group, not only for its monumental size (82¾ by 96⅛ inches) but also for the enrichment of palette and the surface-space intricacies prophetic of the 1930s and '40s. It was one of the last important paintings acquired before the war.[41]

Matisse's search for solidity and construction is manifested in this period by his bronze sculpture, which is also well represented in the Stein collection, beginning with a cast of *The Serf,* 1900–1903 (Plate 13). A derivation from Rodin's *Walking Man* and *John the Baptist Preaching* has often been noted, and though *The Serf* is only half the size of these prototypes, it evidences a search for a more compact and in certain respects more powerful form. It reflects the growing emphasis in Matisse's work on the "essentials of form, the big masses and their relations." The *Woman Leaning on Her Hands,* 1905 (of which one cast is in The Baltimore Museum of Art, Cone Collection), and a blocky little figure, *Small Crouching Nude without an Arm,* 1908? (Mr. and Mrs. Lionel Steinberg Collection, Palm Springs) mark further steps in Matisse's concentration for the sake of that unified rhythm in space he described as the "arabesque." Finally, the charming busts of his two children, *Portrait of Pierre Matisse,* 1905, and that of Marguerite, called *Head of a Young Girl,* 1906 (Mr. and Mrs. Walter A. Haas Collection and Tevis Jacobs Collection, San Francisco, respectively; casts also in The Baltimore Museum of Art, Cone Collection), capture the vitality of a small boy and the meditative gentleness of a young girl.

A number of rare ceramics from about 1907–9 are also worthy of note. In their synthetic, linear style they seem to foretell the decoration of the Chapel at Vence, some forty years later. Among the most representative examples are a vase with figures (Plate 11) and a tile, *Dancing Faun* (John W. Dodds Collection, Stanford).

The collection formed by the Michael Steins after the first World War cannot compare in scope to their earlier acquisitions. A few of Sarah's own paintings, closely inspired by her master, had already joined his work in the Steins' home—further evidence of her identification with him. The two iconlike portraits by Matisse of Michael and Sarah, 1916 (page 34) are perhaps echoes of the artist's trip to Russia in 1911 — especially the one of Sarah, in its almost hypnotic quality, its steely blues and grays, and its contrasted lighting. *The Bay of Nice,* 1917 (Mrs. Madeleine Haas Russell Collection, San Francisco) and *Tea,* 1919 (Mr. and Mrs. David Loew Collection, Beverly Hills), are typical examples of the warmly relaxed attitude, the sunny atmosphere, and the enriched palette and texture of Matisse's painting in the immediate postwar years. The few paintings which the Steins acquired after 1920, such as the *Cap d'Antibes Road,* 1926 (Private collection, Paris), and the *Girl Reading,* 1927 (Brayton Wilbur Collection, Burlingame), mark a continuation of this trend.

The last important act of patronage that Sarah and Michael Stein performed was their creation of a suitable environment for their masterpieces — the Villa Stein (Les Terrasses) erected in 1927 at Garches on the outskirts of Paris by Le Corbusier. He was then a little-known architect whose work Michael is said to

Apartment of Michael and Sarah Stein, 58 Rue Madame, Paris. Early 1908

Above door: MATISSE *Marguerite* (Collection Mrs. Madeleine Haas Russell, Berkeley, Cal.)
First file, top to bottom: MATISSE *Les Gênets* (Collection Mr. and Mrs. Walter A. Haas, San Francisco); MATISSE *André Derain* (Tate Gallery, London); MATISSE *Japanese Woman Beside the Water* (Collection Mrs. Philip Lilienthal, Burlingame, Cal.)
Second file: MATISSE *Red Madras Headdress* (*Mme Matisse*) (Barnes Foundation, Merion, Pa.)
Third file: MATISSE *The Gypsy* (Musée de l'Annonciade, St.-Tropez); MATISSE *Olive Trees* (Private collection, Copenhagen)
Fourth file: MATISSE *Self-Portrait* (Statens Museum, Copenhagen); MATISSE Study for *Joy of Life* (Collection Mr. and Mrs. Walter A. Haas); MATISSE *Reclining Nude, I* (Private collection, Cal.)
Fifth file: MATISSE *Nude Before a Screen* (Collection Robert Ardrey and Helen Johnson Ardrey, Norman, Okla.); MATISSE *Serf* (Art Institute of Chicago)
Sixth file: RENOIR *The Reader* (Baltimore Museum of Art, The Cone Collection); Unidentified painting

have discovered at the International Exposition of Decorative Arts held in Paris in 1925. The pioneering construction of this villa, a rational excursion into the relationship of solids and voids, is close to the spirit of Cubism,[42] and its cool, machine-age aesthetics seem alien to Matisse, though possibly related to his thought in order and clarity. Perhaps the Steins themselves may not have felt altogether at home in their new surroundings, and within the flowing space of the open-plan interior they attempted to re-create with their Renaissance furniture and Oriental objects the warm, cluttered atmosphere of the Paris residences in which they had spent their earlier years. Matisse, however, still reigned supreme on the walls.

The Michael Steins moved back to California in 1935. After Michael's death three years later, his widow rounded off the collection with single prints and illustrated books by Matisse, such as the gracefully linear *Poèmes de Charles d'Orléans* and the syncopated, stenciled patterns of *Jazz* (printed in Paris by Tériade in 1950 and 1947, respectively). But before her death in 1953, Sarah gradually dispersed the collection that she and her husband had once hoped to leave to some public institution in California. During her last years, she still corresponded with Matisse; and in a letter that can be dated about 1946, the painter confided to his old friend:

If my health allows, I shall be able to conclude *in the time I may yet have to live—that is having been born and having started as a colorist (conceiving through*
color), having all my life developed my potential in drawings, requiring so much effort to control my expanding color through the bonds of drawing—I shall end by conceiving through color. . . . Shall I have time to express myself by creating through a union of color and drawing? Express through color that depth of feeling that I have succeeded in giving my drawings?"[43]

In 1955, a Sarah and Michael Stein Memorial Collection was inaugurated at the San Francisco Museum of Art by Mrs. Walter A. Haas and Mr. Nathan Cummings with their respective gifts of the two 1916 portraits of Sarah and Michael referred to above. Mrs. Haas had planned this collection for some time; she had discussed the proposal with Matisse in Paris and had exchanged letters with him about it. Shortly before his death, Matisse chose two drawings and sent them as his tribute to his old friends and patrons; he explained that these drawings "though they seem different, are sure by their qualities to be in perfect harmony with the works of the Stein Collection that may be brought together in the Museum."[44]

Most of the Steins' treasures are now widely scattered. What is the proper epitaph for a once-great collection? "Whether we want to or not," Matisse once declared, "we belong to our time and we share in its opinions, preferences and delusions." Perhaps it is in such a fashion that the collection formed by Michael and Sarah Stein still survives: witness of a former unique moment in the arts, a work of love, and a memorial to a great friendship.

Notes

1   Quoted by Barbara Pollack, *The Collectors: Dr. Claribel and Miss Etta Cone*, New York: Bobbs-Merrill, 1962, p. 270.

2   It is impossible to do justice to the generous assistance encountered in the course of research for the subject of this essay. Mrs. Walter A. Haas should be singled out for originating this project and actively supporting it over the years. We wish to express our gratitude to Mr. and Mrs. Daniel M. Stein for access to family archives. Our special thanks also go to Gerald Nordland, Director of the San Francisco Museum of Art, and Mrs. Anneliese Hoyer, former Curator of Prints; Dr. James D. Hart, Director of the Bancroft Library, and Dr. Richard Bridgman, University of California, Berkeley; Dr. Joseph A. Baird, Jr., of the University of California, Davis, and the California Historical Society; Dr. Donald Gallup, Curator of the Collection of American Literature, Yale University Library, and Miss Janet Flanner, for their encouragement in the early, crucial stages of the research. Among the many helpful friends of the Michael Steins, it is a pleasure to mention particularly Mrs. Elizabeth Bissinger, Mrs. Andrew Cole, Mrs. John L. Stern, Miss Annette Rosenshine, Dr. Maurice Galante, Dr. John W. Dodds, and Professor Keith Crown.

3   In "Testimony against Gertrude Stein," Transition Pamphlet no. 1, The Hague: Servire Press, February 1935 (supplement to *Transition* [Paris], 1934–1935, no. 23), p. 3.

4   *The Making of Americans*, New York: Harcourt, Brace, 1934, p. 43 f.

5   Interview by R. E. Duncan, undated typescript ca. 1955 in Bancroft Library, University of California, Berkeley, p. 29. Alice B. Toklas, who came to Paris in 1907 with her friend Harriet Lane Levy, had met the Michael Steins a year earlier in San Francisco (*ibid.*, p. 26).

6   Gertrude Stein, *The Autobiography of Alice B. Toklas*, New York: Harcourt, Brace, 1933, p. 91.

7   Leo Stein, *Appreciation: Painting, Poetry and Prose*, New York: Crown Publishers, 1947, pp. 140–41.

8   *Ibid.*, p. 102.

9   Gertrude Stein, *Everybody's Autobiography*, New York: Random House, 1937, p. 255; Alice B. Toklas, interview cited in note 5.

10 We thank Mr. Anthony White, a connection of the Crockers, for this account of the acquisition of the painting at some unknown date. As late as 1886, it is listed as in Defoer possession and was subsequently owned by Van Den Eynde (see *Barbizon Revisited*, essay and catalogue by Robert L. Herbert, New York: Clarke & Way, 1962, no. 70; catalogue of an exhibition organized by the California Palace of the Legion of Honor, San Francisco, the Toledo Museum of Art, the Cleveland Museum of Art, and the Museum of Fine Arts, Boston).

11 The E. B. Crockers of Sacramento, cousins of William H. Crocker, had preceded him in collecting activity by a few years. As early as 1885, they established the first art museum in California with the donation of some two thousand paintings and drawings, of uneven quality but wide-ranging interest, which they had acquired in Europe between 1870 and 1872. For this collection and its history, see W. F. Jackson, *Catalogue of Paintings in the E. B. Crocker Art Gallery*, Sacramento: Joseph A. Anderson, 1905, Joseph A. Baird, Jr., "The Crocker Art Gallery," *Art Journal* (New York), Winter 1961/62, pp. 85–88, and B. Lowney, "Lady Bountiful: Margaret Crocker of Sacramento," *California Historical Society Quarterly*, June 1968, pp. 103–4. Other important northern Californian collectors in the 1880s and '90s included Mrs. Phoebe Asperson Hearst, Governor Leland Stanford, and Collis P. Huntington.

12 See e.g., *Catalogue of Paintings Exhibited for the Benefit of the Maria Kip Orphanage and the West Oakland Home for Destitute Children*, arranged by W. K. Vickery, San Francisco, California, 1891 and 1895 (place of exhibition not given).

13 The foundation date is given in the *San Francisco Call Bulletin*, May 10, 1871, p. 3. For the connection of the San Francisco Art Association with the Mark Hopkins Institute, see *Catalogue of Mark Hopkins Institute of Art*, published by the San Francisco Art Association ca. 1900 (no publisher given).

14 An account of the University of California's art activities at this period is given in the *U.S. Art Directory and Year Book*, 1884, p. 61.

15 Mr. Charles Long, Publicity Department, M. H. De Young Memorial Museum, kindly provided this information on the institution's early days.

16 For the consolidation of the street railways on January 14,

1893, see A. H. Schaefer, *Municipal Railroads of San Francisco,* unpublished manuscript of the 1920s in the Bancroft Library, p. 8. According to Alice B. Toklas, the young man accepted his managerial appointment reluctantly and only at the personal insistence of Collis P. Huntington.

17 For stories about Michael's business activities see Stein, *The Autobiography of Alice B. Toklas,* p. 128; Toklas, Duncan interview, p. 13; Harriet Lane Levy, Recollections (untitled, undated, unpaged typescript of about 1950 in the Bancroft Library). Miss Levy, a girlhood friend of Sarah Stein's, had seen the Steins in Paris during an early visit in 1904/5. Her second sojourn in Paris, with Alice B. Toklas, extended approximately 1907 to 1909.

18 Toklas, Duncan interview, p. 14.

19 For an apparently slighting reference to Michael's artistic judgment, see *Journey into the Self: Being the Letters, Papers & Journals of Leo Stein,* edited by Edmund Fuller, New York: Crown Publishers, 1950, p. 19. An example of Michael's actual involvement with the work of Matisse is evidenced in the postcard with a sketch of the *Painter's Family* which the artist sent to him in San Francisco in May 1911 (reproduced in Alfred H. Barr, Jr., *Matisse: His Art and His Public,* New York: The Museum of Modern Art, 1951, p. 153). His grandson Daniel M. Stein states that it was Michael who was later responsible for the choice of Le Corbusier as architect of the Steins' villa Les Terrasses at Garches (see above, p. 44). We thank Mr. Stein for this and other recollections about his grandparents and for communicating family documents referred to here.

20 Annette Rosenshine, "Life's Not a Paragraph," typescript of uncertain date (film in the Bancroft Library), p. 97. Miss Rosenshine relates that she was introduced to Mrs. Stein by Alice B. Toklas during the Steins' visit to San Francisco in 1906, accompanied them on their return trip to Paris, and resided with them until Spring 1908. In 1928 she visited them at Garches.

21 The exact date of this marriage cannot be verified because of the destruction of city records in the San Francisco fire of 1906. It has sometimes been given as 1895, but, as Irene Gordon has pointed out, in an undated letter in the Collection of American Literature at Yale (Beinecke Rare Book and Manuscript Library), which on the basis of external evidence has been dated 1893, Sarah refers to herself as "being newly married."

22 Reference to Sarah Samuels' early art studies is made in Pollack, *op. cit.,* p. 65.

23 "Life's Not a Paragraph," p. 70.

24 Therese Jelenko (née Ehrman), a friend of the Michael Steins' who lived with them in Paris between 1903 and 1905 and visited them on later trips abroad, recalls that a certain amount of swapping took place among the four members of the Stein family in the early days—a custom that has made it difficult sometimes to trace the exact ownership of certain paintings (Jelenko, Reminiscences, untitled, typed transcript of an undated tape recording, ca. 1960, in the Bancroft Library).

25 Ambroise Vollard, *Recollections of a Picture Dealer,* London: Constable; Boston: Little Brown, 1936, p. 136 (translated by Violet M. MacDonald from the original French, *Souvenirs d'un marchand de tableaux*).

26 Levy, Recollections. Vollard adds: "People who came there out of snobbery soon felt a sort of discomfort at being allowed so much liberty in another man's house. . . . Only those who really cared for painting continued to frequent the hospitable house." (Vollard, *Recollections, op. cit.,* p. 137).

27 These reunions are referred to in an undated manuscript note from Matisse's daughter Mme Georges Duthuit to Mrs. Walter A. Haas. The importance of Matthew S. Prichard for the thinking of Matisse is stressed by George Heard Hamilton, *Painting and Sculpture in Europe: 1880 to 1940,* Baltimore: Penguin Books, 1967, p. 107.

28 Levy, *op. cit.,* relates that on that visit, which took place in 1913, Dr. Barnes made the then-generous offer of $5,000 to Michael Stein for one of Picasso's paintings in the Rue Madame, but the offer was refused. Subsequently, however, Dr. Barnes was to acquire two of the Steins' Matisses—the *Blue Still Life,* 1907, and the *Red Madras Headdress,* 1907–8, which they had sold to Tetzen Lund around 1918.

29 Both Therese Jelenko and Annette Rosenshine agree on this from their recollections of living with the Steins in Paris between 1903 to 1905, and 1906 to 1908, respectively. Miss

Rosenshine adds: "They were really poor. They lived meagerly in order to have some surplus to spend on pictures."

30 In a letter of May 25, 1954, to Mrs. Walter A. Haas, Matisse mentions that he had always tried to make special prices for the Michael Steins.

31 Sarah Stein's version of the Stein-Matisse encounter, in which she acknowledges that Leo had been the first of the family to discover Matisse's painting, was related by her late in life to her friend Dr. Jeffery Smith of Stanford University (see Fiske Kimball, "Matisse: Recognition, Patronage, Collecting," *Philadelphia Museum Bulletin,* March 1948, p. 37.

32 Recollections, cited above.

33 "Life's Not a Paragraph," *ibid.* On the dedication page of a copy of André Rouveyre's *Repli* (Paris: Bélier, 1947; now owned by Mrs. Walter A. Haas, San Francisco), which Matisse had designed and illustrated, he wrote on May 25, 1951: "A Madame Michel Stein qui m'a si souvent soutenu dans mes faiblesses."

34 Published as Appendix A in Barr, *op. cit.*, pp. 550–52.

35 This and the quotations that follow are either from Sarah Stein's academy notes, published in Barr, *ibid.*, or from "Notes of a Painter" by Henri Matisse, *ibid.*, pp. 119–23, translated from the original French, "Notes d'un peintre," *La Grande Revue* (Paris), December 25, 1908.

36 For an account of the Gurlitt Gallery exhibition and its aftermath, and a list of the Matisses on loan, see Barr, *op. cit.*, pp. 177–78 and notes 4–6, pp. 540–41.

37 Reminiscences. A resumé of conflicting family claims regarding the purchase of this painting is given in Barr, *op. cit.*, pp. 56–58. Mrs. Haas recalls that during a visit she paid to Matisse in 1953, he told her that the *Woman with the Hat* had always been one of his most cherished works.

38 The sale of this painting is referred to in a letter of Michael Stein to Gertrude, February 1915, published in Donald Gallup, *The Flowers of Friendship, Letters Written to Gertrude Stein,* New York: Knopf, 1958, p. 106.

39 *Ibid.*, p. 37.

40 The *Red Madras Headdress* and *The Hairdresser* (Barr, *op. cit.*, p. 150).

41 This painting can be discerned in the background of several family photographs owned by Mr. Daniel M. Stein. It may be the one regarding which Michael Stein wrote to Dr. Claribel Cone on January 5, 1912, referring to "a great big new decoration about 8 x 10 feet which has necessitated rearranging our room entirely" (*ibid.*, p. 143). For additional references to the *Interior with Eggplants,* see Jean Leymarie, "The Paintings of Matisse," in the catalogue of the *Henri Matisse Retrospective,* University of California, Los Angeles, 1966 (exhibition later shown at The Art Institute of Chicago and the Museum of Fine Arts, Boston), p. 14.

42 The innovative aspects of this house are described by Le Corbusier and P. Jeanneret, *L'Architecture vivante,* Paris: Morancé, 1929.

43 Mr. Daniel M. Stein kindly communicated this letter. Although the first page is missing, it can be dated by its references to Matisse's crippling illness some five years earlier (1941) and his daughter's wartime experiences (1944); cf. Barr, *op. cit.*, pp. 257–58.

44 For this collection, see Grace L. McCann Morley, "The Sarah and Michael Stein Memorial Collection," *San Francisco Museum of Art Quarterly Bulletin,* Series II, vol. IV, no. 2, 1955, pp. 18–23.

PICASSO. *Portrait of Gertrude Stein.* 1905–6.
The Metropolitan Museum of Art, New York,
bequest of Gertrude Stein, 1946

MATISSE, PICASSO AND GERTRUDE STEIN
by Leon Katz

IN THE autumn of 1905, Leo and Gertrude Stein entered decisively into the world of twentieth-century art at a moment of crisis—the furore generated by the exhibition of Matisse's *Woman with the Hat*. An atmosphere of controversy has continued to surround the incident. How the purchase of this painting came about, and which of the four Steins was chiefly responsible for it, are questions that have given rise to conflicting claims and counterclaims. But of the significance of the purchase there can be no doubt. It marked the beginning of the Steins' major influence as collectors and publicizers of the most advanced art being produced in Paris at the time and was also a step toward the international recognition of Matisse as one of the greatest of modern painters.

There can also be no doubt that in the voyage of brother and sister toward the center of the then current revolution in painting, it was Leo who steered the course. Ever since the days of their postgraduate studies at Johns Hopkins University, Leo had been painting and collecting; and under his tutelage Gertrude began first to appreciate Whistler and Leo's collection of Japanese prints, and then—several steps behind—El Greco, Mantegna, Renoir, and the Post-Impressionists, especially Cézanne.

But Gertrude, arriving later, stayed longer. Leo's contempt for Cubist "funny business" and new trends in art grew rapidly after 1911, the year in which the intellectual and emotional break with his sister began, before their parting of ways in 1913. Gertrude, however, remained in close rapport with a succession of artists in Paris—as collector and connoisseur, sometimes as friend, and most importantly as a fellow artist, the development of whose own art paralleled and was influenced by theirs.

During the years from 1906 to 1911 (roughly concurrent with the "heroic" years of Analytic Cubism from 1907 to 1912), Gertrude was chiefly preoccupied with writing her massive novel, *The Making of Americans*.[1] Work on the novel entailed a series of revolutionary aesthetic reorientations on her part, and the attention she paid to painters and painting was almost entirely determined by their relevance, as personalities or as craftsmen, to this private artistic concern. Artists as well as other figures who passed through the salon at 27 Rue de Fleurus were either incorporated into the characterological system she was elaborating for her novel or were studied for their artistic consequence. In her voluminous notes for the book,[2] she gives evidence of the impact that the painting produced in Paris had on her own work, and she records the sometimes aberrant, sometimes profound reflections on artists whose work was being amassed on the walls of the apartment she and Leo Stein shared, and on those of the Michael Steins' on the Rue Madame.

Visitors who came to the Saturday evening "at homes" at the Rue de Fleurus almost never engaged Gertrude's personal interest, but only her quiet attention. Leo explained, and Gertrude watched. Sitting without moving on one of the high-backed chairs in the atelier, speaking only formal phrases to people who approached her, she would remain in silent composure for hours, once in a while bursting into sudden fits of laughter. The greatest impression she made was one of seriousness—an impression that, unknown to her visitors, derived from her concentration on matters that had nothing directly to do with their conversation. Making observations to herself and arranging them into formal schemes was intense and silent work.

That work had begun in earnest when she became familiar with Cézanne's portrait of Mme Cézanne. At Berenson's instigation, Leo had gone to Vollard's in the spring of 1904 for his first look at Cézanne's paintings, and the following summer he discovered the Cézannes in Charles Loeser's house at Florence, where, he says, he spent more time "than I did with the pictures in the Uffizi and the Pitti." After he and Gertrude had returned to Paris, and probably during the winter 1904/5, they bought the *Portrait of Mme Cézanne,* ca. 1881 (now in the Bührle Collection, Zurich),[3] and with that purchase Gertrude began to make a studied response to the painter. Up to that time, she had formed little of her own vision, and none of her predilections concerning art, with any degree of clarity. With her experience of the portrait, the maturation of her own aesthetic began.

Her understanding of Cézanne was strikingly different from that of Leo, who approached him by way of the Italian quattrocento painters. Mantegna's *Crucifixion,* which he once declared was his favorite painting in the Louvre, was for Leo "a sort of Cézanne precursor with the color running all through it." "I was quite ready for Cézanne," he wrote, because of the way of seeing painting he had developed in his study of the Renaissance Italians. His approach focused on the emphasis on color, simplification of forms, and subordination of illustrative interest to purely compositional qualities.

For Gertrude, Cézanne's *Portrait of Mme Cézanne* manifested an altogether revolutionary sense of composition, whose "realism" superseded the reality of the objects represented. As she saw it, Cézanne was treating composition itself as the essential aspect of reality—as the "entity"; and this method of treatment it was incumbent on twentieth-century painters and writers to pursue to its ultimate consequences.

In an interview in 1946, she declared:

... Cézanne ... gave me a new feeling about composition. ... I was obsessed by this idea of composition ... it was not solely the realism of characters but the realism of the composition which was the important thing. ... This ... had not been conceived as a reality until I came along, but I got it largely from Cézanne. Flaubert ... too, had a little of the feeling about this thing, but they none of them conceived it as an entity, no more than any painter had done other than Cézanne.[4]

For Gertrude Stein, Cézanne's particular vision of composition represented a complete break with the traditional sense of structure. In her view, in the *Portrait of Mme Cézanne* the painter rendered every object, and every aspect of each one, as uniformly compelling to his sensibility and uniformly alive to his observation. In this uniformity, any ideational structuring of objects within the frame is eradicated. The center no longer provides the organizing principle; in fact, there is no center and consequently no "frame." Cézanne signified for her a rediscovery of the actual basis of the observer's relation to reality—as uniformly seen, and therefore uniformly meaningful and uniformly emphatic. Thus, Cézanne began what she was to regard as one of the essential struggles of the twentieth century: the effort to flatten significance, to remove those films of hieratic and hierarchical constructs with which Western philosophic tradition had beclouded the field of the observ-

Gertrude Stein in the studio at 27 Rue de Fleurus, Paris. ca. 1905

er's vision. "I believe in reality," she wrote, "as Cézanne or Caliban believes in it. . . . Always and always, Must write the hymn of repetition."

The notion of the decomposed composition that she gleaned from the Cézanne portrait was incorporated directly into her writing. In "Melanctha,"[5] a story she wrote concurrently with her study of the portrait, she undertook programatically to achieve the kind of compositional "reality" in literature that she thought Cézanne had achieved in painting. The "center" of the story, which would normally have been the moment of significant revelation or climax, is instead "distributed" throughout; that is, there *is* no center, and episode is sequential rather than supportive of a climactically centered structure.

GERTRUDE'S RESPONSE to Matisse, during the months following the purchase of the *Woman with the Hat,* when the Matisses became regular visitors both to the Rue de Fleurus and especially to the Michael Steins' at the Rue Madame, was one of respect but not of ardor. Leo immediately recognized Matisse as the most considerable among the artists he had met so far. He felt that as a personality, Matisse was intuitive and intelligent, in contrast to the "witty and cynical" Vallotton, and Manguin, who talked fluently and easily. He admired Matisse also for being religiously conscientious about painting, working endlessly on his pictures, "as persistent as Cézanne himself." Leo conversed with him soberly and intimately about painting; his sister-in-law Sarah became Matisse's altogether devoted disciple.

Gradually, as Gertrude's personal rapport with Matisse disintegrated, her understanding of him became

Gertrude Stein
in the courtyard of 27 Rue de Fleurus, Paris. ca. 1906

more critical and perhaps more complex than that of the other Steins. She accepted his genius as a plain fact and did not waver in this view, even after her devotion to Picasso had supplanted all other artistic devotions, and even after her dislike for Matisse amounted almost to enmity. But as a "person" Matisse seemed to her to have a "singular kind of blindness." It was a blindness that adhered tenaciously to his genuine experience, which he never allowed himself to transform into vapid generalizations or romantic and alienated recollections. His blindness, she noted, made him "slow" and "unreasonable"—slow, in that his attack on the problems of painting had neither the *esprit* nor the grace of Picasso's quick gesture and leap; unreasonable, "on account of the tenacity with which he holds to his central idea [of] himself and his art" and "the dogged persistence of the thing that for the time he knows." Never denying his experience, "in him there is no contradiction, there may be a doubt of it, a terror of losing or having lost it . . . but his whole life is the affirmation of his experience." She discerned that Matisse's sense of himself was much like that of her father—the sense of being "as big as all the world around him"; and in a later notebook entry, when she tried to classify his personality within one or another of the categories in the elaborate psychological system she had devised for *The Making of Americans,* she remarked the peculiar way in which Matisse eluded classification. He was as "mundane" as he was "bohemian." In terms of sexuality, he was as "clean" as he was "dirty." And with regard to his characteristic way of attacking, he was both "murky coward" (as Gertrude classified herself) and irrepressibly and eagerly engaged in "courageous" conflict. He was "so big it don't count."

What gradually infuriated her about Matisse was what she called his "brutal egotism." By this, she did not mean that he shared her kind of self-adulation but simply that, in following his own bent with the overwhelming power and drive of his "unreasonable tenacity," he unconsciously left no room for ordinary civilities. Few of Matisse's associates would ever have conceived of criticizing him for incivility; to all of them he seemed preeminently a man of astonishing correctness, professional in his bearing, bourgeois in his manner, and kindly and forbearing in his relationships. Gertrude, however, took note of trivial instances that for her became significant indications. "Brutal egotism of Matisse shown in his not changing his prices," she wrote, when Matisse in 1909 signed a contract whereby Bernheim-Jeune became his exclusive agent without making any separate arrangement to exempt the Steins, who had been among his first patrons, from paying the elevated prices which his work would henceforth command. On another occasion, in 1910, when Mme Matisse did not share her husband's enthusiasm for his projected trip to Spain, while she would be left behind to take care of the household, Gertrude was amused but chagrined at Matisse's unconscious arm-twisting. "I am content!" Matisse told his wife. "You are not content?" "I am content you are content," she replied. From which Matisse concluded, "You are content? I am content." And he went. This episode was utilized by Gertrude in her "Storyette H.M."[6]

GERTRUDE'S DEFECTION from Matisse was accelerated by what she regarded as the misdirection his painting took, in the years after the *Joy of Life* of 1905–6, and by the absolute commitment she was to make to Picasso, both as person and artist. More and more, Matisse "belonged" to the Michael Steins, while Picasso and his circle filled the atelier at the Rue de Fleurus.

For Leo, the contrast between the solid and conscientious Matisse, surrounded by his family and working with consistent determination, and the waiflike Picasso, living in sordid dinginess with his mistress in the "Bateau Lavoir" in Montmartre, was striking. From Leo's description of his early visits to Picasso, it is clear that he was slightly unsettled by Picasso's illogical and playful temperament. It is equally clear that after Gertrude once took to him, he also decisively took to her.

For years Gertrude was to watch Picasso with the closest attention, worrying over his shifts of mood and what she thought of as his betrayals of his real self. Her notes betray her anxiety as she watches him skirt the traps of his temperament. She is never unsure of her analysis of him; her comments are based on a certainty growing out of complete absorption in his problems—both personal and creative—and complete identification of his struggles with her own.

Gertrude's discernment of Picasso is subtle and various. Seeing him so much in the round, her portrait of him ends by being as critical as it is flattering. She plainly assumes that he is doomed to live permanently with his "Spanish tragedy." What is open to question is whether his character and his deepest nature might in some way permanently cripple or divert his art.

Gertrude thought of Picasso as a "Basarof" (from the character in Turgenev's *Fathers and Sons*). For her, Basarofs possess "reality and arrogance . . . the combination makes them not susceptible of reality in others."

It is important for them to remain opaque in this way, since it is their method of concentrating their experiences and themselves. For such persons, the danger lies in fanaticism, on the one hand, and "dirtiness," on the other. Their fanaticism is dominated by a "mystic idea" that leads them finally to "the denial of their experience . . . it may make them aesthetic visionaries as Raymond [Duncan] & (I hope not) Pablo. Pablo may be saved by the intensity of his actual aesthetic experience, if he can hold to that he will go on." But like Turgenev's Basarof, such assertive and visionary types, no matter how genial, possess a basic core of "*sale*" sexuality. This underlying nature does not necessarily lead to promiscuous and "*sale*" sexual adventure; it can as easily result in rigidity, self-imposed for the sake of controlling and petrifying their sexuality. Though Picasso is the most genial kind of Basarof, Gertrude writes, in his sexual nature he is nevertheless very dirty.

It was her prayer that this extreme of sexuality might counterbalance Picasso's "Basarofian" aesthetic mysticism. In the book she wrote on him in 1938,[7] this original analysis of his temperament is still discernible. She describes the success of his work in terms of self-correction: his alternate natures dominate in turn and provoke their successive contradictions. But essentially, Picasso remains in control of himself. That is to say, neither his sexuality nor his intellect, but his instinctive creativity, is the impelling force of his behavior. She predicates creativity on one's relation to the world rather than to oneself; and in the rare instances in which a human being is more "in existence" in relation to the world than to himself, he approaches genius—or, to put it another way, the condition of complete con-

PICASSO. *Apple.* 1914.
Collection Mr. and Mrs. David Rockefeller, New York

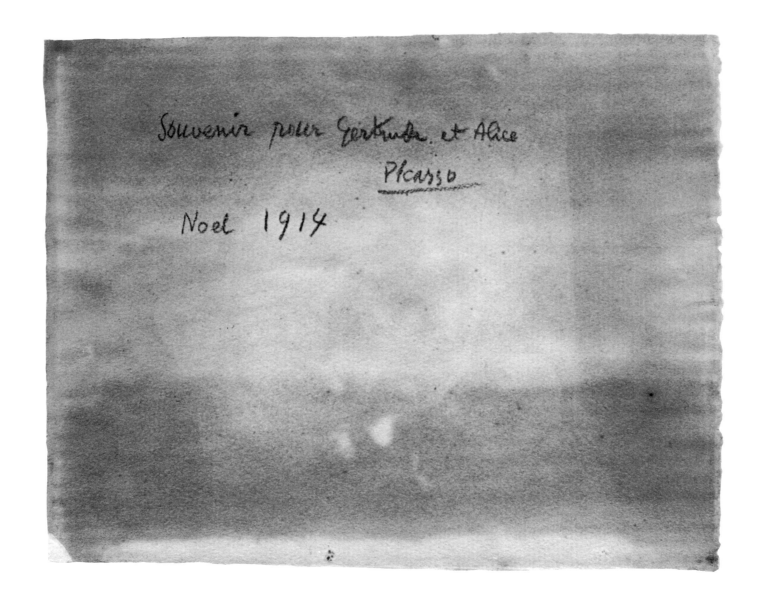

Reverse of watercolor on previous page:
Souvenir pour Gertrude et Alice/ Picasso/ Noel 1914

sciousness. For Gertrude, Picasso represented the greatest instance of its realization that she had ever known.

Because of her certainty of Picasso's genius, she liked for that very reason to dwell paradoxically on his weaknesses. For example, in the section on Picasso in her *Matisse, Picasso and Gertrude Stein*[8] (written in 1910), she planned to describe the "weakness of the genius." Temperamentally, out of weakness, Picasso followed any impulse, because he was incapable of saying no to anything. His response to success was childish; it would sometimes make him fatuous in his behavior and in his opinion of himself. His fantasies were of the kind that grew out of a stupid imagination, the kind that played with such questions as, what would people do if they had wings? His playfulness, childish and innocent, was invariably touched by stupidity. Most paradoxical of all was "his not extremely passionate nature." During the early years when he was living with Fernande Olivier, Gertrude thought she detected, through the maternal quality of Fernande's devotion, his fundamental indifference to her as a woman. His passion and sexual energy were directed, she believed, almost wholly toward his painting.

ONE MUST be cautious in appraising the relation between the art of Picasso and that of Gertrude Stein. In her understanding, their orientation toward the most significant problems of art was identical; but certainly they shared nothing of manner or métier, and the writer's solutions were not based on any imitation of those of the painter. The relationship can be understood initially, perhaps, by recalling Picasso's revision of his *Portrait of Gertrude Stein*, 1906 (page 50), after the "eighty or ninety sittings" Gertrude reports she endured for the original version. The Iberian mask that Picasso substituted for the head continues to resemble Gertrude's face—continues, in fact, to be a portrait in the ordinary way. Yet the recognizable characteristics of the face and head are rendered so severely that they lose all mobility, and the eyes are so generalized that they lack personal expression. The head is at once both Gertrude's head and its reduction to a mask.

The pre-Roman Iberian sculpture exhibited at the Louvre in the spring of 1906 before Picasso left for Spain was the source of this new formality in his work.[9] The ink drawing *Peasants from Andorra* (The Art Institute of Chicago) and the oil painting *Woman with Loaves* (Philadelphia Museum of Art), both done at Gosol in the Spanish Pyrenees during that summer, show the first suggestion of this way of "stating" a portrait. Within the context of these works, the mask becomes both an icon and a "thing" in its own right. The reductive vocabulary of the mask is emphasized to such a degree that, in a sense, device becomes object. Directly after Picasso returned to Paris in the fall and completed the *Portrait of Gertrude Stein* by painting in the new face, he began work on the series of studies which were to culminate in the spring of 1907 with *Les Demoiselles d'Avignon* (The Museum of Modern Art, New York). Here the new masklike portrayal was to reach its ultimate development and, together with other innovations, bring Picasso to the threshold of Cubism.

A year later, in 1908, Gertrude Stein was to reach an equivalent stage of development in her own work. When she reached that stage, the manner of her novel suddenly took a new turn. Without being conscious of it, in the preceding years—a time of many false starts in her writing—she had been moving precisely in the direction heralded by Picasso's painting from the summer of 1906 through 1908: the direction, that is, of inventing an iconography that would describe reality with such pervasive force that it would assume an aesthetic importance within the composition equal to that of the figures or objects being described. Gradually, this insistent iconography becomes not merely the element that subsumes the composition but itself the primary element out of which the composition is made.

Gertrude's bent for psychologically diagrammatic characterization led her to solutions equivalent to Picasso's portraiture. Just as Iberian stone head or African mask were on occasion the basis for Picasso's new iconography, which he then translated into a new formal vocabulary, so diagrammatic psychological relations became Gertrude's essential vocabulary; and relational contexts, even more than the characters described, became the "objects" out of which she composed her novel.

The conjunction of Picasso's and Gertrude's artistic directions is even more apparent in *Les Demoiselles d'Avignon* than in the *Portrait of Gertrude Stein*. It is futile to look for technical correspondences between this major work of Picasso's and Gertrude's work of about the same time—her so-called but misnamed "pre-Cubist" and "Cubist" writing. Yet it is no accident that both artists were then passing through a comparable stage of development, and that those stages of development have comparable significance. Both *Les Demoiselles d'Avignon* and *The Making of Americans* lack firm premises, and the finished form of each is nothing so much as the consequence of successive attempts to discover them. Both display several kinds of expression, sometimes in violent conflict with one another—with the first not obliterated, and the last not pervasively in control of the final work.

To the end of her life, Gertrude thought of Picasso's major painting and her own writing of those years as "ugly" and "brutal" creations that frankly show their record of struggle. Her whole sense of the period, and of the aura that surrounded those heroic years of seminal work, was based on her recognition of the "ugly giants" then being created by Matisse, Picasso, and herself. The "brutality" of each of their works was the outcome of the process that created them—the successive shuckings off of old habits of seeing and rendering, and the ultimate emergence of a new art. The resultant work, however, was never the end of the process, but rather the record of it—the evidence of vigorous, passionately sustained, successive attacks toward the solution of a retreating problem. "Real thinking is conceptions aiming again and again always getting fuller, that is the difference between creative thinking and theorising." The process of creating a work of art and the process of arriving at a whole and central view of reality were for Gertrude one thing. The "form" that all these works take is therefore the accidental result of their being chronological testimonials to the "struggle" to realize the artist's vision. They do not manifest that vision uniformly throughout all their parts; but, facing in its direction, they reach it only at their last stage, in which the making of the composition is brought to a significant halt rather than to a final completion.

To understand the ultimate sense in which Gertrude regarded her own work and Cubist painting as being

Alice B. Toklas and Gertrude Stein
in the studio at 27 Rue de Fleurus, Paris. 1922
(Photograph by Man Ray)

engaged in the same "struggle," we must confront a banal fact. Cubist compositions represent particular objects; every one of them shows specific persons, places, and things. Further, the composition merely represents these, without allegory or emotion, and without any attempt to give them a general significance. No matter how opaque, convoluted, turgid, or disoriented a particular thing may become, it is always *that* thing and no other, nor is it shown in order to exploit it thematically.

This focusing of interest upon the "object as object" is precisely what Gertrude did not find in Matisse for several years from 1905 to 1910, when his large "decorations" were being executed. In these works, as distinct from his portraits and still lifes—and most clearly in the great 1905–6 composition, the *Joy of Life*—figures and faces are treated summarily, and evocations of allusions and emotions dance all over the canvas as forcefully as do the figures represented. Gertrude's distinction between the two kinds of artistic orientation manifested by Picasso and Matisse is fundamental to her concept of art. Matisse's "in-between decorative period," she writes, "was and is a failure." Her whole anxiety concerning Picasso's destiny as an artist is rooted in one essential question: would anything in his makeup interfere with his love of "object as object"? As Picasso's various "styles," "concepts," and "periods" supplant one another, they go unnoticed in the notebooks. One thing, and one alone, rivets her attention: what is Picasso's present "relation to the object"? Naturally, the "ob-

jects" with which she and Picasso were dealing were as different as the difference between the writer's and the painter's concerns. She was concerned with human beings, their patterns of behavior, and their relations; he, with visible phenomena. But her sense of the intensity and impersonality of the painter's and writer's investigation of their respective subject matter is the same; and the dogged, unabating zeal that finally wrests from these different subject matters their "reality" is for her the primary activity that goes on in writing and in painting. The evidence within the work of the realization of that process is the absolute criterion of its excellence. Art that has any intent other than that of bringing the object as object to full realization is to her mind secondary, and art that loses the particular object as its central focus is immoral: "the moment art becomes abstract, it is pornographic." The highest art is the highest realization of the most complex objects: "the final test is always the portrait."

As a passionately involved partisan in the Cubist movement, Gertrude Stein wrested something like a formulation out of that moment's struggles, through which she was able to structure her own. Roughly, her formulation was this. "To kill the nineteenth century," the art of this century—painting and writing—must organize compositions that are "de-centralized" and object-oriented, and that are expressed in a conceptual iconography that itself ultimately becomes the object of the composition.

Notes

1 Although completed in 1911, *The Making of Americans* did not find publication until it was serialized in *transatlantic review,* April-December 1924; the following year it was brought out in book form (Paris: Contact Editions).

2 Gertrude Stein's notes and studies for *The Making of Americans* are in the Collection of American Literature, Beinecke Rare Book and Manuscript Library, Yale University. Quotations from them are used here with the permission of Yale University Library and the estate of Gertrude Stein. See the present author's "The First Making of *The Making of Americans:* A Study Based on Gertrude Stein's Notebooks and Early Versions of the Novel (1902–8)," Ph.D. dissertation, Columbia University, 1963.

3 Also known as *Mme Cézanne Seated in an Armchair* and *La Dame à l'éventail.* The painting had been among those included in the Cézanne retrospective at the 1904 Salon d'Automne. It may be seen in the photograph reproduced on p. 61.

4 William S. Sutton taped this interview in Paris, on the basis of questions submitted from America by Robert Bartlett Haas in preparation for an anthology to be called *A Primer for the Gradual Understanding of Gertrude Stein.* It was subsequently transcribed and published in three installments: Robert Bartlett Haas, "Gertrude Stein Talking—A Transatlantic Interview," *Uclan Review* (Los Angeles: University of California), Summer 1962, pp. 3–10; Spring 1963, pp. 40–48; and Winter 1964, pp. 46–48. The excerpt quoted here appears in the first installment, pp. 8–9. A note preceding the final installment states that the date of 1945 previously given for the interview is incorrect; it actually took place on January 5 and 6, 1946.

5 Included in *Three Lives,* written 1905–6; first publication New York: Grafton Press, 1909.

6 *Portraits and Prayers,* New York: Random House, 1934, p. 40: "He came in all glowing. The one he was leaving at home to take care of the living was not glowing. The one that was going was saying, the one that was glowing, the one that was going was saying then, I am content, you are not content, I am content, you are not content, I am content, you are content, I am content, you are content, I am content."

7 Gertrude Stein, *Picasso,* Paris: Floury, 1938; English edition, New York: Scribners; London: Batsford, 1939.

8 *Matisse, Picasso and Gertrude Stein with Two Shorter Stories,* Paris: Plain Edition, 1933.

9 This was first pointed out by James Johnson Sweeney, "Picasso and Iberian Sculpture," *Art Bulletin* (New York), September 1941, pp. 191–98.

Juan Gris. Paris, 1922 (Photograph by Man Ray)

GERTRUDE STEIN AND JUAN GRIS
by Douglas Cooper

"WE WERE intimate," writes Gertrude Stein in "The Life of Juan Gris. The Life and Death of Juan Gris," a memorial "portrait" of the artist which was published two months after his death.[1] And "intimate" they must have been for a few years in the mid-1920s. However, it is difficult to assemble enough evidence to reconstitute the reality of the friendship between Gertrude and Gris, "one of her two dearest friends,"[2] because this seems to have been largely intellectual and on both sides is sparsely documented.

When and how did Gertrude Stein and Juan Gris meet? We do not know. Gertrude did not record the date and neither Picasso nor Kahnweiler remembers anything about it. All that is certain is that they already knew each other in February 1914 when Josette went to live with Gris in the "Bateau Lavoir." But Gris had been living there since 1906 and was a friend of Picasso's, whom Gertrude often visited there in his studio, so the two might have met at any time between 1907 and 1914. But we know that no real friendship developed between them in these early years because Josette remembers that they were not "intimate" even in 1914. Confirmation of this seems to be further provided by the first surviving letter from Gris to Gertrude, a postcard from Collioure dated July 31, 1914, which begins formally "Ma chère Mademoiselle." The only indication Gertrude gives of her early awareness of Gris occurs in *The Autobiography of Alice B. Toklas*, in which she says: *It was in these days that Juan Gris, a raw rather effusive youth came from Madrid to Paris and began to call Picasso cher maître to Picasso's great annoyance. It was apropos of this that Picasso used to address Braque as cher maître, passing on the joke . . .*[3]

There is doubt, however, as to the date implied by "in these days," because Gertrude/Alice leaps around in her time references. In the preceding paragraph she is writing about the use of "printed letters" in Cubist painting, which implies the years 1911–12. In the line preceding the reference to Gris she says that "in these days . . . the intimacy between Braque and Picasso grew," which implies 1909–10; while her succeeding paragraph opens with the statement "But I am once more running far ahead of these early Paris days when I first knew Fernande and Pablo." Now, since she refers here to three landscapes brought back by Picasso after a summer in Spain (i.e., Horta de San Juan) as being at the "beginning of cubism," this should relate to the fall of 1909. But Alice Toklas did not go to live with Gertrude Stein until the summer of 1910.[4] Weighing up the evidence, therefore, we may deduce that Gertrude and Gris probably met in 1910 or 1911, that is to say, after Picasso had left the "Bateau Lavoir."

On the other hand, Gertrude cannot have begun to see or like Gris's painting until much later. In the *Autobiography* she states clearly: "It was just two months before the outbreak of the war that Gertrude Stein saw the first Juan Gris paintings at Kahnweiler's and bought three of them."[5] That must mean that she had not seen Gris's first small show at Sagot's in Montmartre in January 1912, nor his *Portrait of Picasso* and other paintings at the Salon des Indépendants in March 1912, nor those at the Section d'Or exhibition in October 1912. Indeed, she even claims that "the first serious exhibition of his pictures" occurred at the Galerie Kahnweiler, Rue Vignon,[6] in 1914. Now Kahnweiler had made a contract with Gris at the end of 1912 to buy all his output, so it is strange that Gertrude, who liked to go to the gallery to look over the newly acquired paintings, had not seen works by Gris in 1913. It is also strange that she should have mistaken looking at paintings in a showroom for an exhibition. But she did give the correct date for her first purchases, *Glass and Bottle*, 1913–14, and *Book and Glasses,* 1914, because a letter to her from Kahnweiler dated June 3, 1914, exists,[7] in which he wrote: "I have today sent to you the two paintings by Gris and now enclose the bill for them. I am delighted that these paintings have been added to your collection." Presumably Gertrude purchased her third Gris of 1914, *Flowers* (Plate 24) between that date and the latter half of July, when she herself left for London and Kahnweiler closed his gallery. By these purchases, Gertrude Stein became one of a small group of connoisseurs who had already felt the impact of Gris's painting before the outbreak of war and had begun to buy his works. And Gris was never to forget what her support and encouragement at this time meant to him.

Gertrude Stein, who had been in close contact with Picasso since 1906, and also knew Braque, was one of the first enthusiastic supporters of true Cubist painting. This she felt specially privileged to understand and appreciate not only because "americans can understand spaniards," but also because she had made up her mind that "cubism is a purely spanish conception and only spaniards can be cubists."[8] Her discovery of the Cubist paintings of Juan Gris, another Spaniard, confirmed her in this quixotic belief.

The next episode in the story of Gertrude and Gris, though it was to have disastrous consequences, shows Gertrude trying to be a generous friend and patron as well as a shrewd collector. By September 1914 Gris, who was still with Josette at Collioure, was virtually without money and, owing to the war, was not receiving what was due him under his contract with Kahnweiler who, as a German, had taken refuge in Italy. Picasso, hearing of Gris's plight, sent him a small sum, Matisse too helped him, and on October 26 Gris gratefully acknowledged by letter a postal order of 200 francs sent by Gertrude Stein at the suggestion of Picasso. This kindly gesture proved to be the beginning, however, of an unnecessary "quarrel" between Gertrude and Gris.

In mid-September, Gris received a letter from Paris from Michael Brenner who, with his partner Coady, ran the Washington Square Gallery in New York. Brenner was seeking Kahnweiler's address because he wanted to buy some paintings to show in New York. Gris had met Brenner a year previously at Céret, and Brenner had then bought a painting from Kahnweiler. So Gris, who had a number of new works unsold in his studio, quickly forwarded the letter to Kahnweiler, hoping that he might allow him to sell something directly and get money. Kahnweiler had not answered by October 30 when Gris, penniless, worried, and therefore unable to work, wrote to him a second time to say that Matisse had in the meantime talked with Gertrude Stein and Brenner in Paris and arranged that he, Gris, should receive 125 francs per month between them in exchange for paintings. "I don't think they expect to get them at the same price as yourself," he told Kahnweiler, "because that would not suit you any more than it would me. Given the present state of affairs, I suppose you will have no objections." With a little money in hand,

Gris and Josette then returned to Paris at the beginning of November.

But Kahnweiler objected vigorously to this arrangement,[9] interpreting Gris's action as an attempt to sell paintings behind his back and threatening to proceed against him for breach of contract. Gris, stunned and uncomprehending, wrote again to say that he would only be "lending" the paintings to Brenner temporarily and that, with regard to sales, Kahnweiler should "make [his] own arrangements with [Brenner] after the war." He even pleaded:

The financial assistance which I am getting from Brenner at the moment is simply a loan to enable me to live and go on working. I can't see what harm it can possibly do to you if I, a Spaniard, exhibit in America some pictures which I have painted even though they are morally your property. Nor can it be in any way against the law, for neither of us is French, and the pictures cannot legally become the property of your gallery until they have been labeled and entered in your books.

By November 13 Gris was telling Kahnweiler that Gertrude was "willing to help to the extent of 50 frs. per month as agreed and on the conditions you propose," and that he should write at once to Brenner, because he too would probably accept the same arrangement. But Kahnweiler remained adamant in claiming that he alone had the right to dispose of Gris's paintings, which belonged to him by virtue of their contract. As a result, by Christmas 1914 Gertrude and Brenner had become so "cross" over the shilly-shallying and having to pay out money without getting pictures in return that, before leaving for the front in an ambulance corps, they canceled their financial aid and broke abruptly with Gris. To add to his worries, Gris then found that he had "nothing whatever to live on" but felt morally obliged to repay to Gertrude and Brenner the sums he had received from them, 500 francs in all. Gertrude later replied that her 200 francs had been "a gift." However, Gris had no alternative than to write to Kahnweiler to tell him that it was now his responsibility to send him regular remittances of money, beginning immediately via his sister who lived in Madrid. And this remained Gris's only source of income until he began to sell to Léonce Rosenberg early in 1916.

The quarrel between Gertrude and Gris lasted throughout the war years. Josette does not remember Gertrude ever coming to the studio at that time, no letters were exchanged between Gertrude and Gris, and between July 1914 and June 1921 Gertrude acquired none of his paintings. Yet in the *Autobiography* she never mentions this breach but claims in a passage dealing with life in Paris in 1916:

It was in these days too that the friendship between Gertrude Stein and Juan Gris began. He was living in the rue Ravignan . . . We used to go there quite often. Juan was having a hard time, no one was buying pictures . . . Juan was in those days a tormented and not particularly sympathetic character. He was very melancholy and effusive and as always clear sighted and intellectual. He was at that time painting almost entirely in black and white and his pictures were very sombre. . . . His situation was desperate.[10]

By this time, Gris had been freed a year previously by Kahnweiler and was about to sign a new contract with Léonce Rosenberg, so if Gertrude had felt inclined, she could easily have helped Gris out of a "desperate" situation by buying paintings. But she obviously felt that he was not "sympathetic" and perhaps did not like his work at that time. In any case, the most convincing proof that they did not patch up their quarrel and become friends again during the war is provided by his next letter to her, dated February 2, 1920, the tone of which is reserved and formal:

Dear Miss Stein:

I am greatly flattered by what you say about my contribution to the Indépendants, more especially as I have a great respect for your understanding of painting.

Thank you very much. I hope I shall have a chance of seeing and talking to you.

Yours very sincerely and devotedly
Juan Gris

From this point on, however, a real friendship did start to grow up between Gertrude and Gris, and within three years they were "intimate." After 1920 the character of Gris's painting changed radically, its former austerity and precision being replaced by a more lyrical suavity. But this seems to have appealed to Gertrude who, after the reopening of Kahnweiler's gallery (renamed Galerie Simon) in September 1920, resumed her old habit of going there regularly to look at Gris's latest paintings. Before his death she had purchased the following examples for her collection: *The Table in Front of the Window,* April 1921, bought June 8, 1921, exhibited at Galerie Simon in 1923 as *La Fenêtre devant l'olivier,* and again in 1928 as *L'Olivier*; *Seated Woman,* 1924, bought in the fall of 1924; *The Green Cloth,* 1925, bought in June 1925; *Dish of Pears,* 1926, bought in the fall of 1926 (Plate 25).

By April 1921 Gris was already seeing quite a lot of Gertrude, and during the next few years, whenever he was well and in Paris, he was a frequent visitor to her apartment on the Rue de Fleurus. At the end of April 1921 they met in Monte Carlo, where Gris was doing some work for Diaghilev's ballet. A few days later Gertrude and Alice Toklas spent two days with Gris at Bandol, where he was recuperating from his first serious illness, to discuss collaboration on some ballet project which came to nothing. By November 1921 Gris was at last writing to Gertrude as "Ma chère amie"; while his remark in a letter to Kahnweiler of February 13, 1922, "Gertrude Stein has not written to me as you said she would. Yet I would have liked to know what she thinks about the pictures," shows how much he had come to rely on her artistic judgment. And this is re-emphasized by two letters to Gertrude, in which Gris writes:

I'm rather satisfied with my latest pictures and I'm curious to know what you think about them. (December 27, 1922);

and again, just before his first one-man exhibition at the Galerie Simon:

I am working hard to finish some pictures I have begun. As I have about ten here, I would like to show them to you before they are exhibited. (February 27, 1923)

Presumably, since she bought nothing from this exhibition, Gertrude was not captivated by Gris's painting in 1922-23, yet this did not mar the course of their rapidly growing friendship. While Gris was again working for Diaghilev at Monte Carlo in October–December 1923, he and Gertrude often exchanged visits, Gris going to see Gertrude in Nice and she coming to his studio in Monte Carlo. After one of these visits Gris wrote to Kahnweiler (November 5, 1923) that Gertrude thought his latest paintings "very pretty," and added significantly: "That has encouraged me because I wasn't sure of them."

Throughout the period 1922–24 Gris struggled with his new style of painting while his own feelings about it fluctuated, though it seemed to him that on the whole he was making progress. But, as he told Gertrude in a letter of October 10, 1924, "my lack of success makes me very uncertain and I have no confidence in anything." One way in which Gertrude chose at this time to return Gris's affection and respect for herself was to try to make his name better known and encourage others to buy his paintings. In August 1922 Gertrude sent a Boston journalist, Kate Buss, to see Gris and write an article about him for the American press. Then in August 1924, having prevailed upon *The Little Review* to feature the work of Juan Gris in a future number, Gertrude sent Jane Heap, its editor, to look at paintings in his studio and promised to write about them herself. Gris was delighted and wrote to Gertrude that "no one will write better about my painting than yourself." The result was the short text in which her admiration, informed understanding, and real friendship inspired such pertinent and characteristic passages as: *Juan Gris is a Spaniard. He says that his pictures remind him of the school of Fontainbleau* [sic]. *The school of Fontainbleau* [sic] *is a nice school, Diana and others. In this he makes no mistake, but he never does make a mistake. . . . He is a perfect painter painter* [sic], *alright, he might be right. . . .*

Juan Gris is one is the one who combines perfection with transubstantiation. By this he lives to say to-day yesterday and to find a day.

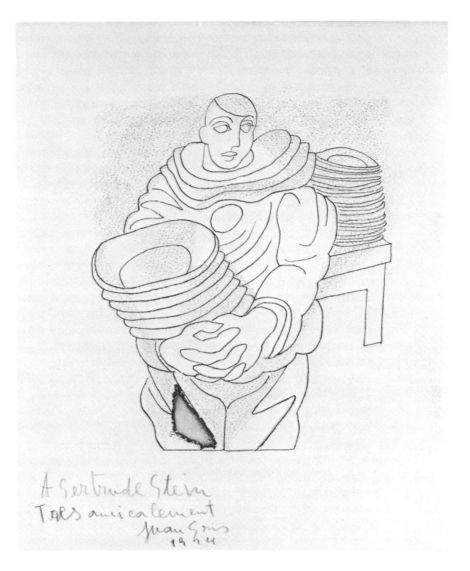

GRIS. *The Clown.* 1924.
Collection Mr. and Mrs. Lionel Steinberg,
Palm Springs, California

Let me tell all I know about Juan Gris.

To begin with he has black thoughts but he is not sad. To begin with he is complete and not completed. To begin with he is necessary and not destroyed....[11]

The period of true intimacy in the friendship between Gertrude Stein and Juan Gris seems to run from 1923 till his death in 1927 and to gain in intensity each year. In April 1924 Gris turned to Gertrude first of all for approval of the text of his important analytical and aesthetic statement *Des Possibilités de la Peinture,* a formulation of his own pictorial methods and beliefs, which he was to deliver as a lecture before an audience of members of a philosophical society at the Sorbonne in May. In a letter of October 1924, thanking Gertrude for her piece about his paintings in *The Little Review,* Gris sounded a new note of trust and friendship: "Thank you very much indeed, my dear Gertrude. This has been an enormous consolation to me in my present state of despondency." At this time too Gris had the additional consolation of learning that Gertrude had begun once more to buy his paintings. Shortly afterward he presented Gertrude with the drawing of a clown (page 69), which had served as a preparation for a lithograph illustration in *Le Casseur d'Assiettes,* a book by Armand Salacrou that was published by Kahnweiler in December 1924. Then at the beginning of 1925 Gris presented Gertrude with his rejected design in watercolor of a boat deck (page 71), made for the stage setting of "a short ballet with decor and costumes to last not more than 15 minutes," which he had been asked to prepare in September 1924 by Varna, manager of the Casino de Paris. In the summer of 1925 Gris specially chose the painting *The Green Cloth,* which Gertrude

had recently bought, to represent him in the L'Esprit Nouveau pavilion, designed by Le Corbusier, at the Exposition des Arts Décoratifs in Paris. At this time he also designed covers for chairs and stools in Gertrude's home which were executed in needlework by Alice Toklas. Then during 1926 Gris worked on the four lithograph illustrations for Gertrude's *A Book Concluding with As a Wife Has a Cow, A Love Story,* which was published by Kahnweiler in December 1926. But Gertrude and Gris cannot have seen much of each other during this final year of his life because Gris was absent from Paris until mid-April 1926; Gertrude was away from July until the end of October; Gris left for Hyères at the end of November and when he came back to Paris in February 1927 he was already a dying man. Nevertheless they carried on an active and affectionate correspondence. And after Gris's death in May 1927, which left Gertrude Stein "heart broken,"[12] she wrote "The Life and Death of Juan Gris" for *Transition,* which she was subsequently to describe as "the most moving thing" she ever wrote.

Here Gertrude began by contrasting Gris's resentment of "the lack of trust and comradeship in Spanish life" and his dislike of "Spanish ways" with his "very great attraction and love for french culture." "It seduces me and then I am seduced over again," she writes, quoting his own words. After which Gertrude goes on:

And this being so and it is so Juan Gris was a brother and comrade to every one being one as no one ever had been one. That is the proportion. One to any one number of millions. . . . Josette equable intelligent faithful spontaneous delicate courageous delightful forethoughtful the school of Fontainebleau delicate deliberate meas-

GRIS. *Boat Deck*. 1924.
Collection Nelson A. Rockefeller, New York

ured and free all these things seduced. I am seduced and then I am seduced over again he was fond of saying. He had his own Spanish gift of intimacy. We were intimate. Juan knew what he did. . . . As a Spaniard he knew cubism and had stepped through into it. He had stepped through it. There was beside this perfection. To have it shown you. Then came the war and desertion. There was little aid. Four years partly illness much perfection and rejoining beauty and perfection and then at the end there came a definite creation of something. This is what is to be measured. He made something that is to be measured. And that is that something.

Therein Juan Gris is not everything but more than anything. He made that thing. He made the thing. He made a thing to be measured. . . . And he liked a knife and all but reasonably. This is what is made to be and he then did some stage setting. We liked it but nobody else could see that something is everything. It is everything if it is what is it. Nobody can ask about measuring. Unfortunately. Juan could go on living. . . . I remember he said Kahnweiler goes on but no one buys anything and I said it to him and he smiled so gently and said I was everything.[13]

This text is a deeply felt expression of Gertrude's "permanent and vital"[14] interest in Gris and conveys something of her feelings about his personality. But it tells us nothing significant about what she saw and liked in his painting. As a matter of fact, Gertrude never wrote anything as meaningful about Gris as she did about Picasso, though in *The Autobiography of Alice B. Toklas,* which was published six years after "The Life and Death," she included a few comments which are revealing. There she remarks that "the only real cubism is that of Picasso and Juan Gris. Picasso created it and Juan Gris permeated it with his clarity and his exaltation."[15] Then, drawing a comparison with her own writing, which Gertrude felt was an inalienable part of Cubism, she continues:

Gertrude Stein, in her work, has always been possessed by the intellectual passion for exactitude in the description of inner and outer reality. She has produced a simplification by this concentration, and as a result the destruction of associational emotion in poetry and prose. She knows that beauty, music, decoration, the result of emotion should never be the cause, even events should not be the cause of emotion nor should they be the material of poetry and prose. Nor should emotion itself be the cause of poetry or prose. They should consist of an exact reproduction of either an outer or an inner reality.

It was this conception of exactitude that made the close understanding between Gertrude Stein and Juan Gris.

Juan Gris also conceived exactitude but in him exactitude had a mystical basis. As a mystic it was necessary for him to be exact. In Gertrude Stein the necessity was intellectual, a pure passion for exactitude. It is because of this that her work has often been compared to that of mathematicians and by a certain french critic to the work of Bach.[16]

This sounds well until one reads Gris's own writings on his pictorial aims and methods and considers those of his paintings which Gertrude chose to acquire for her collection. She began well without a doubt, but then she passed over all his work done between 1915 and 1920, perhaps the only period in connection with which it is reasonable to evoke "clarity," "exaltation," and "exactitude." It is difficult to identify these as the outstanding qualities of *Seated Woman* or *Dish of Pears,* while of *The Table in Front of the Window* Gris himself wrote in a letter to Kahnweiler (April 9, 1921): "It is much looser in execution and has a sort of popular look which I rather like, but which is not due to using popular means. It has, if I'm not mistaken, a sort of Derain air."

But one should not look for serious art criticism in the writings of Gertrude Stein. What mattered most to Juan Gris was her friendship, her admiration for his work, their animated artistic discussions, and her stimulating mind.

Notes

Quotations from Juan Gris's letters are taken from *Letters of Juan Gris,* collected by Daniel-Henry Kahnweiler, translated and edited by Douglas Cooper (London: Privately printed, 1956).

1   In *Transition* (Paris), no. 4, July 1927, pp. 160–62; reprinted in an amended version, which is used here, in Gertrude Stein, *Portraits and Prayers,* New York: Random House, 1934, pp. 48–50.
2   *The Autobiography of Alice B. Toklas,* New York: Harcourt, Brace, 1933, p. 111.
3   *Ibid.,* p. 112.
4   Alice Toklas is generally said to have moved into Gertrude's home at 27 Rue de Fleurus in the fall of 1909. In fact, this did not occur until August 1910: the evidence is to be found in letters from Leo Stein to Gertrude (August 1910; Collection of American Literature, Beinecke Rare Book and Manuscript Library, Yale University, hereafter given as "Yale") and from Claribel Cone to her sister Etta (September 20, 1910; Cone Archives, The Baltimore Museum of Art). I am grateful to Irene Gordon for providing me with this information.
5   *Autobiography,* p. 132.
6   *Portraits and Prayers,* p. 49.
7   (Yale).
8   *Autobiography,* p. 111.
9   Like many other people at the time, Kahnweiler was falsely optimistic about the outcome of the war and saw himself resuming his dealing activities in Paris within six months. By the spring of 1915 he had to face reality and, being himself short of funds, then canceled his contract with Gris.
10 *Autobiography,* pp. 195–96.
11 "Juan Gris," *The Little Review* (New York), Autumn and Winter 1924-25, p. 16; reprinted in an amended version as "Pictures of Juan Gris," in *Portraits and Prayers,* pp. 46–47.
12 *Autobiography,* p. 260.
13 *Portraits and Prayers,* pp. 49–50.
14 *Autobiography,* p. 258.
15 *Ibid.,* p. 111.
16 *Ibid.,* p. 259.

Claribel Cone, Gertrude Stein, and Etta Cone.
Florence, June 1903

THE CONE SISTERS AND THE STEIN FAMILY
by Ellen B. Hirschland

NO SOONER had Leo and Gertrude Stein moved to Baltimore in 1892 than they found ready acceptance into a congenial circle of young intellectuals, among whom two sisters, Claribel and Etta Cone, were to become their lifelong friends.[1] The friendship blossomed when Gertrude returned to Baltimore from Radcliffe in 1897 and entered Johns Hopkins Medical School, where Dr. Claribel Cone was doing research in pathology, simultaneously holding a professorship at the Woman's Medical College of Baltimore. The study of medicine was an unusual pursuit for women at that time, so there was a natural kinship between Gertrude and Claribel, though the doctor was ten years older. But actually, it was Etta Cone, just four years Gertrude's elder, who became her intimate friend, as is evidenced by their joint travels during the following decade in America and in Europe, and by the warm correspondence between them, much of which has been preserved. The correspondence was frequent up to the first World War and continued on a more casual basis into the 1930s.

The Cone sisters' father died in 1897, leaving each of his eleven surviving children an inheritance with a modest, yet comfortable annual income.[2] Etta, thus independent, journeyed to Europe with two friends in 1901. Leo Stein, who had been living abroad for several years, surprised them by meeting them upon their arrival in Naples. That same day they all set out to visit the National Museum. Subsequently, the foursome traveled to Pompeii, Capri, Sorrento, Rome, and on to Leo's beloved Florence. He enjoyed teaching, and Etta in particular was a devoted pupil. The entries in her journal indicate a ready response to the art treasures that were then still so new to her. On June 16 she wrote:

... [we] went to the Academy for our second visit and I was delighted with dear old Botticelli's Allegory of Spring ... The old Madonna of Cimabue 13th cen. also one of his pupil Giotto. Read some of my legends of Saints by Mrs. Jameson. Leo met us at the gallery and came back to lunch with us after which we ... went to the Boboli Gardens belonging to the Pitti Palace. I have never seen more beautiful gardens, the long shady walks being wonderfully arranged, the trees seeming to touch the sky. In some of these arcades the trees overlap above and in others they are trained apart. A most unique grotto at the entrance has some very effective marble statues in the rough by Michael Angelo. This place though unusual did not attract me....[3]

Leo spent nearly a month showing the three young women around, before he left on his own travels. Later in the summer, they joined him and Gertrude in Paris where members of the group spent almost every day together, usually searching for Japanese prints. Etta bought quite a few of these as well as some "perfectly irresistible bookplates" that she and Gertrude found. Etta also hunted "antiquities" and was occupied with visits to the Louvre and to the couturiers. "Gertrude and Hortense went with me ... to pass judgment on a hat for me. Gertrude liked it, so I ordered it."[4]

Two years later, in 1903, both sisters traveled to Europe. Claribel was bound later in the season for the Senckenberg Institute in Frankfurt-am-Main, where she would study off and on during the next three years. On Etta's arrival in Florence, she found a letter from Gertrude inviting her to come to Rome. When Etta declined, Gertrude came instead to Florence where they all took long walks in the hills and had warm and intense discussions. Etta's diary records some impressions: *... at the Santa Maria Novella ... we saw much but stopped short in front of Uccello's foreshortened God, on the picture of the Flood in the cloister. Stayed until church closed. Then walked over to the Maddelein dei Pazzi to see Perugino's crucifixion in the Chapter house there. ... took omnibus for the Santa Maria del Carmine. Enjoyed the Massaccio's ... Began to feel the enormous difference in tactile values between Filippino Lippi's & Masolino's in the same chapel here. We then went to the San Spirito, which is a beautiful church & found a Filippino Lippi ...*[5]

The following year Etta returned to Europe, sailing from New York with Gertrude early in June. At Genoa they met Claribel, who had come from Germany to join them, and the three proceeded to Florence where they met Leo. He had recently discovered the work of Cézanne through Bernard Berenson and had also learned that Charles Loeser, an American living in Florence, owned a number of Cézanne's paintings. It can be presumed that Leo spoke to the women of Cézanne, about whose work he was so enthusiastic.

During the winter of 1905/6 Etta, now thirty-five years old, rented an apartment in Paris at 58 Rue Madame.[6] Leo's and Gertrude's elder brother Michael and his wife Sarah lived with their young son Allan in the same building, a short walk from the home of Leo and Gertrude on the Rue de Fleurus. Etta explored the city, took piano lessons once or twice a week, and typed Gertrude's first novel, *Three Lives,* from the handwritten manuscript.

That season many exciting events were to take place for Etta. In October the Steins purchased *Woman with the Hat* (Mr. and Mrs. Walter A. Haas Collection, San Francisco), their first painting by Matisse, at the Salon d'Automne. The Cone sisters attended the opening of the exhibition, after which Claribel left for Germany. A few months later, on February 18, 1906, Etta noted the purchase "1 water color, 1 drawing Matisse."[7] During this period she also bought the *Yellow Pottery from Provence,* her first oil painting by Matisse.[8] These were the first of the forty-three paintings, eighteen pieces of sculpture, and numerous drawings and prints by Matisse covering the period 1895–1947 which were eventually to form the nucleus of the Cone Collection.

Shortly after the purchase of *Woman with the Hat,* Leo was introduced to the work of Picasso by Clovis Sagot, a picture dealer and vendor of artists' supplies. Leo and Gertrude became frequent visitors to Picasso's studio, taking Etta with them. At Picasso's request she gave him the comic section of an American newspaper,[9] in exchange for which she was invited to help herself to the sketches and etchings lying about on the floor. Etta's sense of propriety made her reimburse Picasso for these drawings and prints. Her expense notebook,[10] on November 2, 1905, lists "1 picture 1 etching Picasso" for 120 francs (then the equivalent of approximately $23). In the spring she began to purchase his work in earnest: the entry for March 3, 1906, notes 11 drawings and 7 etchings for 175 francs (about $34). According to Gertrude, when Claribel accompanied her sister to the studio, Picasso referred to the two sisters as "The Miss Etta Cones."[11]

Late in 1906 the Cone sisters began a year-long journey around the world with their oldest brother and his wife. Back home in America, Etta was pleasantly sur-

prised one day when she opened a letter from Gertrude
and found enclosed a self-portrait of Picasso doffing his
hat, inscribed "Bonjour Mlle Cone." Etta wrote back
to Gertrude:

*A funny coincidence—here I am at my desk having
come to tell you that it was about time for you to be
writing to me, and here comes your dear old letter with
this delightful sketch of Picasso and Fernando's [sic]
wishes. Dey sure am nice folk and I hope to see them in
the near future, so thank them for their respects and
please give them mine and tell Pablo that Fernando
ought massage his tummy into shape again. I love his
picture for it is just like him.*[12]

During the next four years, Stein-Cone reunions took
place in Paris and Florence; in between, the correspondence flourished. In the summer of 1912, while traveling in England, Etta wrote to Gertrude from Cambridge:
*Sister C. has a new method of seeing cathedrals. [E.g.]
Ely Cathedral. She goes through with her umbrella
open over her. And her umbrella has only one half its
surface covered, the other half has slipped away from
the ends, because needle and thread are no longer of
avail in holding it to the proper places.*

*Now the reason why my sister goes through Ely
Cathedral with her umbrella raised, is because several
bats have selected the Ely Cathedral as the scene of
their wanderings also.*

You can picture the scene.[13]

Over the years Gertrude had been writing word "portraits" of her friends. In 1912 she completed "Two
Women," a dual portrait of the Cone sisters, whom Gertrude named Martha [Claribel] and Ada [Etta]:[14]

. . . They were large women, both of them, anybody

PICASSO. *"Bonjour Mlle Cone."* 1907.
Ink on paper, 8¼ x 5½".
The Baltimore Museum of Art, The Cone Collection

could see them. They were large women either of them. Very many saw them. Very many saw each one of them. Some saw them. Really not very many saw them, saw both of them. They were large women. Really not very many saw both of them. And that was a natural thing. There were two of them. They were together and they knew it then. They were not together and they knew it then. They were both large women and they were very different the one from the other of them, very different, and one, Ada, was younger and called her sister, sister Martha, and one, Martha was older and called her sister Ada.[15]

Gertrude's characterization of the sisters as "large women" is apt. The immediate impact on seeing them was one of stateliness and noble dignity. Claribel was the shorter and the heavier of the two, but as both grew portly, they resembled each other more. They had strong features and were handsome in an unromantic way. Etta's face was monumental and pensive, with a straight, rather severe mouth, a strong nose, and heavy black eyebrows which later on contrasted strikingly with her ample, pure white hair. She resembled somewhat the Gilbert Stuart image of George Washington.

Claribel's appearance was majestic. She held her head aloft and seemed to radiate a kind of intangible superiority, dominating her surroundings. She wore her long hair plaited, with flat braids rolled round and round, held in place with a bone comb. Into her coiffure she usually stuck a silver skewer, which served double duty as a letter opener.

A divergence in taste had developed between the sisters, as is evidenced by their championship of different cultures. Scientifically, Claribel was oriented to-ward Germany where she studied for so many years, and she felt comfortable with the people and the language. Etta spoke French fluently, albeit with an American accent, and preferred the French people and their way of life. In this regard, she was somewhat closer than Claribel to the Steins and their interests.

Dr. Claribel was the extrovert who, with her imperious appearance and conduct, was the more conspicuous of the two sisters, but it was Etta who was always studying art and whose response was deeper and more personal. In fact, she was the first among this group to buy paintings. As early as 1898, when Claribel and Gertrude were occupied with their medical studies, Etta acquired five paintings by Theodore Robinson at a posthumous auction of his work in New York. With her choice of this American Impressionist, Etta Cone showed an early propensity for French painting and began the collecting of art, which was to be the principal endeavor of her life from then until her death half a century later. In her modest way she acquired a profound knowledge of the history and quality of painting and sculpture as well as laces, brocades, furniture, drawings, prints, books, and jewelry. She went beyond the lessons of the Steins, yet she, along with Claribel, delighted in purchasing art objects that had belonged to them.

During World War I, the Michael Steins and Gertrude and her friend Alice Toklas stayed in France; Leo and Etta were in America; and Claribel resolutely remained in Munich, almost completely oblivious to world events. When she finally returned to Baltimore in 1920, Claribel was delighted to discover that the Cone Mills had grown into a dominant enterprise in the cotton in-

Gertrude Stein, Etta and Claribel Cone.
Vallombrosa, July 1903

dustry, increasing what had been a nest egg into a sizable fortune.

In 1922 the sisters began making annual trips to Europe, and the Stein-Cone reunions resumed. The Cones were now more active collectors, purchasing works of art from a number of dealers as well as from the Steins. On June 6, 1925, for example, Michael Stein wrote that the Cones had arrived in Paris and had already bought some of Gertrude's possessions. "I also spoke to them about the Laurencin and they seemed interested."[16] A few days later he could write Gertrude, "The Laurencin is sold for 10.000."[17] The painting bought from Gertrude for $2,150 is Marie Laurencin's *Group of Artists* of 1908—a self-portrait with portraits of Apollinaire, Picasso, and Fernande Olivier (Plate 26). It may have been at this time that Etta purchased Renoir's *The Reader* from Sarah Stein.[18] That same summer of 1925, at the Gangnat sale, Claribel bought a major Cézanne oil, *Mont Ste.-Victoire Seen from Bibémus Quarry*, for the then enormous sum of 410,000 francs (on the day of the sale the equivalent of $18,860), the highest price that either sister ever paid for any painting.

The following year, Claribel once again demonstrated her bold taste. At the public auction of the John Quinn estate in Paris, in October 1926, she outbid everyone for Matisse's controversial *Blue Nude* of 1907 (Plate 17). In 1913, when the Armory Show had moved from New York to Chicago, a copy of this painting had been burned in effigy. The audacity of a lady in making such a purchase in the mid-1920s is hardly diminished by reason of the fact that she had often seen the picture during the years it had hung in Leo's and Gertrude's home. Among her purchases from Gertrude that summer was Vallotton's portrait of Gertrude, painted in 1907. In July, Etta bought from Gertrude the small Cézanne *Bathers* (Plate 20), one of the first paintings Leo and Gertrude had purchased in the early years of the century.

The question arises why so many Stein paintings and objects found their way into the collections of the Cones. During the early Paris years when Etta and Claribel were introduced by Gertrude and Leo to Picasso, Matisse, and the art world in general, they probably still felt somewhat insecure in their own taste and judgment. Furthermore, the acquisitive sense of the two sisters and their comfortable financial circumstances provided Gertrude and Leo with an opportunity to place some of their own objects into the hands of the Cones whenever a financial need arose. It is evident that Etta assisted Gertrude financially even before the war. On May 16, 1906, she wrote to her from Germany: "By the way, don't you need some more cash, don't hesitate, and you needn't luxuriate in the feeling of poverty, for its no use to."[19]

After the war, the sisters estimated their annual income and made budgets for their yearly art acquisitions. Thus, it was important for them to buy astutely. They knew the art market and were careful as far as prices were concerned. By now their relationship to the Steins had changed. In the 1920s the friendship was not only based on an identity of taste, philosophy, and sentimental reminiscence but became, largely, an acquaintance of convenience. When members of the Stein family were in need of ready cash, which was often the case, it seemed natural for them to turn to Claribel or Etta to

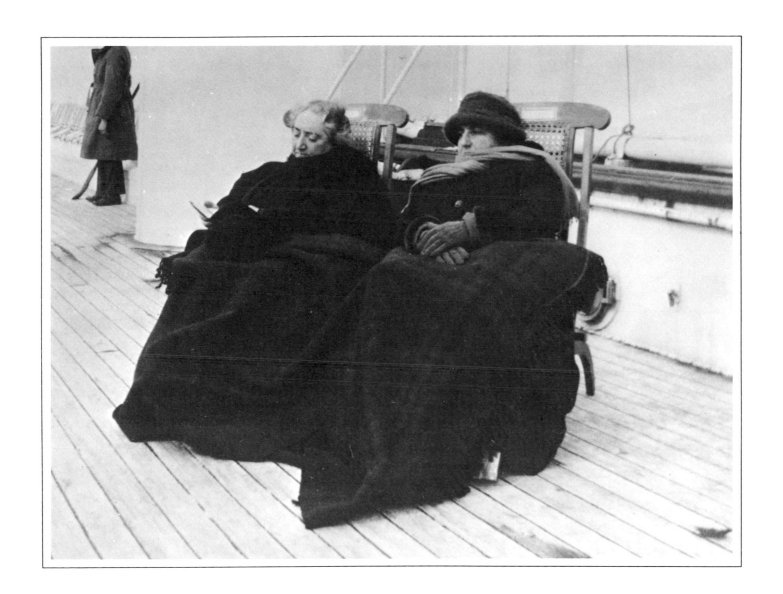

Claribel and Etta Cone aboard the S.S. *Rotterdam*, ca. 1928

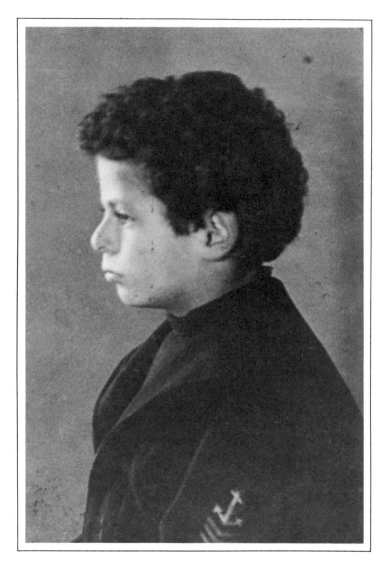

Allan Stein. San Francisco, ca. 1903?

find out whether either of them might be interested in acquiring a Picasso or a Matisse, a Cézanne, a manuscript of Gertrude's, or a piece of antique furniture. By the same token, the Cones were usually delighted to have objects from the Stein collection; after all, they had confidence in their friends' taste and considered the provenances of the paintings above question. Whatever bargain was struck, from the Steins' point of view the price achieved was undoubtedly better than could have been reached by selling the art object to a dealer, and there was an immediate cash payment. An additional advantage to the Steins was the discretion with which a deal of this nature could be accomplished. On the buyers' side, the Cone sisters undoubtedly had the advantage of paying a price that was lower than any a dealer would have asked.

Turning to the leading personalities of the two families, one finds remarkable similarities between Gertrude and Claribel. Gertrude's Saturday night open houses are well known. According to the Baltimore *Evening Sun*, "Dr. Cone's Saturday night parties . . . came as near to forming a salon as anything that this city has ever known. . . . To them came clever people in every walk of life—musicians, artists, writers, scientists —and the discussions which ensued sparkled with wit and wisdom."[20] Etta, obviously aware of the similarity, wrote to Gertrude, ". . . it is a tossup as to which, you or Sister Claribel, likes the being lionized the most."[21]

Like Gertrude, Claribel never practiced medicine. She continued her research in pathology throughout most of her life and published a number of scholarly articles; she enjoyed telling the story that she had had but one single patient in her entire career. Both Ger-

PICASSO. *Portrait of Allan Stein.* 1906.
The Baltimore Museum of Art, The Cone Collection

trude and Claribel had enchanting voices and mesmerized their audiences by their melodic way of speaking. In 1923 Claribel wrote from Paris to Etta in Venice: *Then did I tell you of going home with G & A and reading aloud one of her latest—called an "Elucidation" I said "Elucidation—but does it elucidate!" "However it is very pretty!" "Isn't it!" Gertrude said with satisfied amplitude. Amplitude is the word—I think "satisfied amplitude" is a good Gertrudism for something she has written and sits in her chair listening to with great satisfaction beaming from her face and her whole ample form—so she listened with "satisfied amplitude"—do not forget this expression and some day—if you remember it for me—I shall ask G whether this is worthy—from her point of view—to take its place in the new literature. She quoted at length passages from Shakespeare not nearly so clear as hers—she said. It* may be true.[22]

Years later, Gertrude was to write: "Dr. Claribel Cone of Baltimore . . . loved to read Gertrude Stein's work out loud and she did read it out loud extraordinarily well."[23]

Claribel Cone died in Lausanne on September 29, 1929. As soon as she heard of the death, Gertrude wrote to Etta:

My very dear Etta,

I have just had word from Mike of the death of Claribel and it has saddened me terribly. I was awfully attached to her, oddly enough just the other day we were telling that delightful story of Claribel and the box in her room with the two old bon bons and the Bolsheviks in Munich, everything she did had an extraordinary quality all her own. I had not seen so much of her in recent years but she made a very important and rather wonderful part of my Baltimore past, and Dr. Marian Walker and I were talking of it all and of her in it when she was here just a couple of months ago, and so strangely enough Claribel had been very near me this last summer, and now Etta you know how I understand your loss and feel for it, do take my love and my fondest thought of Claribel.

Always,
Gertrude[24]

A few years later, in Claribel's memory, Gertrude sent Etta a typescript of "Two Women." Etta thanked her and wrote that she would catalogue it among Claribel's art books.[25]

According to the terms of Claribel's will, her collections of paintings, sculpture, textiles, furniture, and other *objets d'art* were left to Etta, to be given to the Baltimore Museum if "the spirit of appreciation of modern art in Baltimore becomes improved."[26] Eventually, Etta did decide to bequeath everything in the joint collections to Baltimore. Meanwhile, with her fortune supplemented by the inheritance from Claribel, and with greater personal assurance, she embarked upon an enormous expansion of her own collection, strengthening it immeasurably. Within the next years she would purchase, among others, Corot's *The Artist's Studio,* Manet's *Lady with a Bonnet,* Gauguin's *Woman with Mango,* Picasso's *Mother and Child,* Matisse's *Pink Nude.* In fact, she bought an important new Matisse almost every year directly from the artist. In 1932 she purchased from Gertrude the portrait of Leo (page 12) that Picasso had painted in 1906.[27]

Etta seriously considered buying Picasso's 1905 *Boy Leading a Horse* (Plate 36), which was once owned by

Leo and Gertrude. In 1936, each morning for an entire month she visited the Rosengart Gallery in Lucerne, viewing the painting and pondering its acquisition.[28] Upon her return to Baltimore, Etta measured her rooms and found that the painting was too high (86½ ") to be hung in her apartment. With great reluctance, she had to decide against its purchase. Subsequently she bought Picasso's *La Coiffure* of the same year.

Although Gertrude's and Etta's correspondence remained warm until its termination in 1934, their lives had gradually drifted apart. On the other hand, the relationship between Etta and the Leo and Michael Stein families remained constant. In 1949, Allan Stein, the son of Michael and Sarah, telephoned Etta in North Carolina from Paris to say that he was ill and in urgent need of funds. He offered her the portrait Picasso had painted of him in 1906 (page 83), the year she had been Allan's neighbor and had taken him on outings to the Luxembourg Gardens around the corner from their home. She was delighted at the idea of owning the painting, and the deal was concluded over the transatlantic telephone. Fate, however, prevented her from enjoying her new acquisition; just a few hours before the delivery of the letter announcing the safe arrival of the portrait in New York, Etta Cone died.

And so the museum in Baltimore, the city in which the Stein-Cone friendship had begun, became the repository for paintings and sculpture and furnishings that had been enjoyed throughout the lives of both families.

Notes

I wish to thank Donald Gallup, Curator of the Collection of American Literature, and the staff of the Beinecke Rare Book and Manuscript Library of Yale University, for the time and help they have so generously given me. The Cone Archives at The Baltimore Museum of Art have also been made available to me, and I should like to express my special gratitude to the staff there for their assistance on many occasions during the course of my work on The Cone Collection.

1 Contrary to legend, there was no family relationship between the Steins and the Cones.
2 While their father was still living the eldest brothers took over and expanded his small wholesale grocery and textile business and established a cotton mill in North Carolina. Through the years they added other mills in the South, in which they concentrated on denims, flannels, printed fabrics, broadcloth, and corduroy.
3 Etta Cone's 1901 journal, now in the Cone Archives at The Baltimore Museum of Art (hereafter given as "Baltimore"). All quotations have been transcribed as they appear in the original.
4 *Ibid.*, entries for September.
5 Etta Cone's 1903 diary, entry for June 18 (Baltimore).
6 Letter of Moses Cone, February 16, 1906, addressed to Etta Cone, in care of Mme Vernot, 58 Rue Madame (owned by Ellen B. Hirschland). In the notebook Etta Cone kept of her

expenses for 1903–6 (Baltimore), she recorded her weekly payments to Mme Vernot for "pension" and piano lessons.

7 Entry in the expense notebook (Baltimore).

8 *Yellow Pottery from Provence,* alternately referred to as *The Yellow Jug,* has generally been dated 1906, but on at least two separate occasions Etta Cone said that she bought the painting in 1905: to Fiske Kimball ("Matisse: Recognition, Patronage, Collecting," *Philadelphia Museum Bulletin,* March 1948, p. 39), and to her cousin Ella G. Ulman ("The Cone Collection," *Right Angle* [The American University, Washington, D.C.], April 1949, p. 2). *Yellow Pottery from Provence* may be the still life exhibited at the 1905 Salon as no. 716, *Nature morte.*

9 The oft-told story that Etta Cone gave Picasso comic strips from the Baltimore *Sun* would seem to be inaccurate, since that newspaper claims that it carried no "funnies," daily or Sunday, until the year 1911. However, in a letter of December 11, 1905, to Mabel Foote Weeks, Leo Stein refers enthusiastically to "an American weekly publication . . . the Comic supplement of the Journal" (Collection of American Literature, Beinecke Rare Book and Manuscript Library, Yale University, hereafter given as "Yale").

10 (Baltimore).

11 *The Autobiography of Alice B. Toklas,* New York: Harcourt, Brace, 1933, p. 64.

12 Etta Cone to Gertrude Stein, letter of January 7, 1908 (Yale).

13 *Ibid.,* letter of July 23, 1912 (Yale).

14 Notes on the manuscript (Yale) leave no doubt as to the identity of the character.

15 The handwritten copy (Yale) has the older sister named "Bertha"; the change to "Martha" was indicated the first time it appeared and was then carried out consistently in the typescript.

16 Michael Stein to Alice B. Toklas (Yale). The letter is dated merely "June 6th." The year of this letter, as well as that of others in the Michael and Sarah Stein correspondence at Yale University, has been determined jointly by Irene Gordon and the author.

17 Michael Stein to Gertrude Stein, letter postmarked June 14, 1925 (Yale).

18 In a letter to Etta of August 20, 1927 (Baltimore), Claribel refers to Etta's purchase of the painting from Sarah Stein as a past event, describing it as a "little corseted female now sitting over your mantel at home."

19 Etta Cone to Gertrude Stein (Yale).

20 *Evening Sun* (Baltimore), April 8, 1911.

21 Etta Cone to Gertrude Stein, letter of March 25, 1913 (Yale).

22 Claribel Cone to Etta Cone, letter of August 13, 1923 (Baltimore).

23 *Autobiography,* p. 154.

24 This undated letter (published in Barbara Pollack, *The Collectors: Dr. Claribel and Miss Etta Cone,* New York: Bobbs-Merrill, 1962, p. 197) is probably of October 1929, since there is a reply from Etta Cone dated November 5, 1929 (Yale).

25 In her letter of thanks of September 14, 1932 (Yale), Etta refers to a "manuscript." However, Gertrude sent a typescript, which was subsequently given to Yale University.

26 *The Sun* (Baltimore), November 22, 1929.

27 Etta Cone to Gertrude Stein, letter of September 14, 1932 (Yale).

28 The author accompanied her on these visits.

27 RUE DE FLEURUS, 1906–1914/15

THE PAIRS of photographs that appear on the following pages reproduce the corners to the left and right of the stove in the studio of Leo and Gertrude Stein. They illustrate the growth of the collection over a period of years—from early in 1906, when Leo Stein first mentions paintings hanging "two deep," to the winter of 1914/15, some months after Leo and Gertrude Stein divided their joint collection.

Studio of Leo and Gertrude Stein, 27 Rue de Fleurus, Paris. Early 1906

Top row, left to right: Manguin *Standing Nude* (Private collection, New York); Bonnard *Siesta* (National Gallery of Victoria, Melbourne); Picasso *Young Girl with a Basket of Flowers* (Collection Mr. and Mrs. David Rockefeller, New York); Delacroix *Perseus and Andromeda* (Baltimore Museum of Art, The Cone Collection)

Bottom row: Cezanne Study for *The Smoker* (Barnes Foundation, Merion, Pa.); Renoir? *Land-scape*; Daumier *Head of an Old Woman* (Henry Pearlman Foundation, New York); Picasso *Head of a Boy* (Owned by the artist); Denis *Mother in Black* (Collection D. Denis, St.-Germain-en-Laye)

Studio of Leo and Gertrude Stein, 27 Rue de Fleurus, Paris. Early 1906

Top row, left to right: CEZANNE *Portrait of Mme Cézanne* (Bührle Collection, Zurich); Painting by Leo Stein?; RENOIR *Two Women* (Barnes Founda-tion, Merion, Pa.); MATISSE *Woman with the Hat* (Collection Mr. and Mrs. Walter A. Haas, San Fran-cisco); TOULOUSE-LAUTREC *The Sofa* (Museu de Arte Moderna, São Paulo); CEZANNE *Bathers* (Bal-timore Museum of Art, The Cone Collection)
Below: Portraits of Michael Stein by Leo Stein

Studio of Leo and Gertrude Stein, 27 Rue de Fleurus, Paris. About 1907

Top row, left to right: PICASSO *Boy Leading a Horse* (Collection Mr. and Mrs. William S. Paley, New York); PICASSO *Dozing Absinthe Drinker* (Collection Ottmar Huber, Glarus, Switz.); PICASSO *Young Acrobat on a Ball* (Pushkin Museum, Moscow); Painting by Leo Stein?; VALLOTTON *Reclining Nude* (Whereabouts unknown)

Bottom row: PICASSO *Seated Woman in a Hood* (Staatsgalerie, Stuttgart); PICASSO *Woman with Bangs* (Baltimore Museum of Art, The Cone Collection); Unidentified painting; PICASSO *Two Women at a Bar* (Collection Walter P. Chrysler, Jr., New York); MATISSE *Yellow Pottery from Provence* (Baltimore Museum of Art, The Cone Collection); DENIS *Mother in Black* (Collection D. Denis, St.-Germain-en-Laye); CEZANNE Study for *The Smoker* (Barnes Foundation, Merion, Pa.)

Studio of Leo and Gertrude Stein, 27 Rue de Fleurus, Paris. About 1907

Top row, left to right: PICASSO *Standing Female Nude* (Collection Mr. and Mrs. William S. Paley, New York); Florentine Madonna; PICASSO *Portrait of Gertrude Stein* (Metropolitan Museum of Art, New York); MATISSE *Corsican Landscape* (Whereabouts unknown); MATISSE *Standing Figure* (Barnes Foundation, Merion, Pa.); MATISSE Study for *Joy of Life* (Barnes Foundation); MATISSE *Small Jar* (Barnes Foundation)

Middle row: PICASSO *Boy with a Milk Can* (Collection Mrs. Oveta Culp Hobby, Houston); MATISSE *Woman with the Hat* (Collection Mr. and Mrs. Walter A. Haas, San Francisco); MATISSE *Olive Trees* (Robert Lehman Collection, New York); MANET *Ball Scene* (Collection Johann Mustad, Göteborg, Sweden); RENOIR *Woman in a Fur Hat* (Barnes Foundation)

Bottom row: PICASSO *Two Nudes* (Museum of Fine Arts, Houston); PICASSO *Head of a Young Man* (Cleveland Museum of Art); PICASSO *Head of a Boy* (Owned by the artist); DAUMIER *Head of an Old Woman* (Henry Pearlman Foundation, New York); RENOIR? *Landscape*

Studio of Leo and Gertrude Stein, 27 Rue de Fleurus, Paris. About 1913

Top row, left to right: MATISSE *Joy of Life* (Barnes Foundation, Merion, Pa.); VALLOTTON *Reclining Nude* (Whereabouts unknown); PICASSO *Seated Nude* (Musée National d'Art Moderne, Paris); PICASSO *Woman with a Fan* (Collection the Honorable and Mrs. W. Averell Harriman, Washington, D.C.)

Middle row: MATISSE *Olive Trees* (Robert Lehman Collection, New York); PICASSO *The Reservoir, Horta* (Collection Mr. and Mrs. David Rockefeller, New York); PICASSO *Still Life* (Collection Mr. and Mrs. John Hay Whitney, New York); PICASSO *Houses on a Hill, Horta* (Collection Nelson A. Rockefeller, New York); PICASSO *Landscape* (Collection Mr. and Mrs. David Rockefeller); PICASSO *Young Girl with a Basket of Flowers* (Collection Mr. and Mrs. David Rockefeller)

Bottom row: 3 watercolors by Cézanne; PICASSO *Head of a Young Man* (Collection André Meyer, New York); 2 obscured works and an unidentified painting

Studio of Leo and Gertrude Stein, 27 Rue de Fleurus, Paris. About 1913

Top row, left to right: MATISSE *Music (Study)* (Museum of Modern Art, New York); PICASSO *Seated Woman in a Hood* (Staatsgalerie, Stuttgart); PICASSO *Young Acrobat on a Ball* (Pushkin Museum, Moscow); PICASSO *Standing Female Nude* (Collection Mr. and Mrs. William S. Paley, New York)

Second row: MANGUIN *Standing Nude* (Private collection, New York); PICASSO *Two Women at a Bar* (Collection Walter P. Chrysler, Jr., New York)

Third row: DAUMIER *Head of an Old Woman* (Henry Pearlman Foundation, New York); PICASSO

Still Life with Glasses and Fruit (Private collection, New York); PICASSO *Portrait of Gertrude Stein* (Metropolitan Museum of Art, New York); PICASSO Study for *Nude with Drapery* (Collection Mr. and Mrs. John Hay Whitney, New York); PICASSO *Violin* (Private collection, New York); PICASSO *The Little Glass* (Private collection, New York); CEZANNE *Portrait of Mme Cézanne* (Bührle Collection, Zurich); CEZANNE *Landscape with Spring House* (Barnes Foundation, Merion, Pa.)

Fourth row: RENOIR *Brunette* (Collection Mr. and

Mrs. Nelson R. Kandel, Baltimore); MANET *Ball Scene* (Collection Johann Mustad, Göteborg, Sweden); CEZANNE *Man with a Pipe* (Collection the Honorable and Mrs. W. Averell Harriman, Washington, D.C.); PICASSO *Still Life with Fruit and Glass* (Collection Mr. and Mrs. John Hay Whitney); CEZANNE *Bathers* (Baltimore Museum of Art, The Cone Collection)

Bottom row: Unidentified paintings and drawings, among them 4 Cézanne watercolors

Studio of Gertrude Stein, 27 Rue de Fleurus, Paris. Winter 1914/15

Top row, left to right: PICASSO *Two Women at a Bar* (Collection Walter P. Chrysler, Jr., New York); MATISSE *Woman with the Hat* (Collection Mr. and Mrs. Walter A. Haas, San Francisco); PICASSO *Woman with a Fan* (Collection the Honorable and Mrs. W. Averell Harriman, Washington, D.C.); PICASSO *Portrait of Gertrude Stein* (Metropolitan Museum of Art, New York); PICASSO *Landscape* (Collection Mr. and Mrs. David Rockefeller, New York); PICASSO *Woman with Bangs* (Baltimore Museum of Art, The Cone Collection); PICASSO *Standing Female Nude* (Collection Mr. and Mrs. William S. Paley, New York)

Middle row: PICASSO *Head* (Collection Nelson A. Rockefeller, New York); PICASSO Study for *Nude with Drapery* (Collection Mrs. Maurice L. Stone, New York)

Bottom row: PICASSO *Still Life with Glasses and Fruit* (Private collection, New York); PICASSO *The Blue House* (Collection André Meyer, New York); PICASSO *The Reservoir, Horta* (Collection Mr. and Mrs. David Rockefeller); PICASSO *Houses on a Hill, Horta* (Collection Nelson A. Rockefeller); PICASSO *Landscape* (Owned by the artist); PICASSO *Vase, Gourd, and Fruit on a Table* (Collection Mr. and Mrs. John Hay Whitney, New York)

Studio of Gertrude Stein, 27 Rue de Fleurus, Paris. Winter 1914/15

Top row, left to right: PICASSO *Man with a Guitar* (Collection André Meyer, New York); PICASSO *Woman with a Mirror* (Art Institute of Chicago); CEZANNE *Mont Ste.-Victoire* (Collection Norton Simon, Cal.); CEZANNE *Mont Ste.-Victoire* (Louvre, Paris); PICASSO Study for *Nude with Drapery* (Collection Mr. and Mrs. John Hay Whitney, New York); CEZANNE *Portrait of Mme Cézanne* (Bührle Collection, Zurich); PICASSO *The Little Glass* (Private collection, New York); PICASSO *Guitar on a Table* (Collection Nelson A. Rockefeller, New York); PICASSO *Still Life with Ace of Clubs* (Collection Mr. and Mrs. John Hay Whitney)

Bottom row: PICASSO *Student with a Pipe* (Collection Nelson A. Rockefeller); CEZANNE *Woods* (Whereabouts unknown); CEZANNE *Footpath in the Woods* (Whereabouts unknown); PICASSO *Violin* (Private collection, New York); MANET *Ball Scene* (Collection Johann Mustad, Göteborg, Sweden); PICASSO *Still Life with Glasses and Fruit* (Collection Nelson A. Rockefeller); PICASSO *Cut Pear, Grapes, and Pipe* (Private collection); PICASSO *Still Life with Fruit and Glass* (Collection Mr. and Mrs. John Hay Whitney)

MORE ADVENTURES
by Leo Stein

These recollections of Matisse and Picasso were written in the 1940s, a few years before Leo Stein's death. They are reprinted here, by permission, from his *Appreciation: Painting, Poetry and Prose,* published by Crown Publishers, New York, copyright 1947 by Leo Stein.

IT WAS later in the year I met Matisse that I met Picasso. I had known for some time in the Rue Lafitte a little dealer, an ex-clown with a pointed beard and bright eyes and a hat pushed back on his head, who twinkled with enthusiasm whatever was the subject, but especially when that subject was Zan or current painting. Zan was a particular brand of licorice which was different from any other and the only one that had the properties of a life preserver. He would interrupt the talk on modern art to put a bit of Zan between his teeth and commend its virtues; then we were back again on the latest show, the latest artistic scandal, the prospects for the future. There was a Spaniard whose works he lauded, and as he had done me some favors I bought a little Spanish watercolor; but when he recommended another Spaniard, I balked.

"But this is the real thing," he said. So I went to the exhibition, and in fact this was the real thing. Besides the pictures, there were some drawings for which I left an offer, since there was no one in charge of the show, but from this I heard nothing further. When, a few days later, I dropped in at Sagot's to talk about Picasso, he had a picture by him, which I bought. It was the picture of a mountebank with wife and child and an ape. The ape looked at the child so lovingly that Sagot was sure this scene was derived from life; but I knew more about apes than Sagot did, and was sure that no such baboon-like creature belonged in such a scene. Picasso told me later that the ape was his invention, and it was a proof that he was more talented as a painter than as a naturalist.

Soon after, I learned that a friend, Pierre Roché, knew Picasso. Roché, a tall man with an inquiring eye under an inquisitive forehead, wanted to know something more about everything. He was a born liaison officer, who knew everybody and wanted everybody to know everybody else. He introduced me to the literary band at the Closeries des Lilas —Jarry, Moreas, Paul Fort and others who had recently made literary history—and once a month or so he came to see me, to tell his news and hear mine. We talked the whole night through. I was always having ideas, and as the same neurosis that kept me from painting kept me from writing also, it was nice to have someone like Roché, who was more ear than anything else. He was delighted to know that I had seen the work of Picasso, and a few days later led me to the Rue Ravignan.

One could not see Picasso without getting an indelible impression. His short, solid but somehow graceful figure, his firm head with the hair falling forward, careless but not slovenly, emphasized his extraordinary seeing eyes. I used to say that when Picasso had looked at a drawing or a print, I was surprised that anything was left on the paper, so absorbing was his gaze. He spoke little and seemed neither remote nor intimate—just quite completely there. The impression he made was satisfying. He seemed more real than most people while doing nothing about it. The atelier was a mess. There was a heap of cinders beside the round cast-iron stove, which was held together with a twisted wire (it later burst); some crippled furniture; a dirty palette; dirty brushes; and more or less sloppy pictures. Long after many of the pictures had become mine, Picasso came to the house one day with his paint box and cleaned them up. Later Vollard bought a bunch of them on condition that he should do the same for him, but I believe he never did.

The homes, persons and minds of Picasso and Matisse were extreme contrasts. Matisse—bearded, but with propriety; spectacled neatly; intelligent; freely spoken, but a little shy—in an immaculate room, a place for everything and everything in its place, both within his head and without. Picasso—with nothing to say except an occasional sparkle, his work developing with no plan, but with the immediate outpourings of an intuition which kept on to exhaustion, after which there was nothing till another came. The difference in mental type between Picasso and Matisse came out vividly in a later incident.

At Durand-Ruel's there were at one time two exhibitions on, one of Odilon Redon, and one of Manet. Matisse was at this time specially interested in Redon, because of his own work and because of friendship with the older man, who was then in difficulties. When I happened in he was there, and spoke at length of Redon and Manet, with emphasis on the superior merits of the lesser man. It was quite common for Matisse, whose mind was not rigid, to overflow in some direction because of a temporary interest. He told me he had seen Picasso earlier, and Picasso had agreed with him. This seemed to me improbable. Picasso's appreciations did not have this fluidity, and he had no special interest in Redon. However, there was no reason to say this, so I let it pass.

Later on that same day Picasso came to the house and I told him what Matisse had said about Redon and Manet. Picasso burst out almost angrily, "But that is nonsense. Redon is an interesting painter, certainly, but Manet, Manet is a giant." I answered, "Matisse told me you agreed with him." Picasso, more angrily: "Of course I agreed with him. Matisse talks and talks. I can't talk, so I just said *oui oui oui*. But it's damned nonsense all the same." Picasso, though often influenced by others, was not so openly receptive as Matisse was.

Matisse was a social person rather than a convivial one. Picasso was more convivial than social. Matisse felt himself to be one of many, and Picasso stood apart, alone. He recognized others, of course, but as belonging to another system. There was no fusion. Matisse exhibited everywhere.

He always wanted to learn, and believed there was no better way than to see his work alongside the work of everybody else. Picasso never showed with others. It was partly diffidence, partly pride. Once at a salon he said to me, "I don't see how these fellows can exhibit this stuff; of course my work is bad too, but then I know it"; after a moment, "Perhaps they know it too, but they show because it's the best they can do."

Renoir once said, "I want to remain in the ranks"—something Picasso could never have said. He felt himself a man apart—what the story books call a man of genius, though not pretentiously so. But in those days he was not sure. He was not aggressive, but felt the right to be aggressive. Once we were waiting for places in an omnibus, and many went on. After the passengers with lower numbers than ours had mounted, Picasso burst out, "This is not the way it ought to be. The strong should go ahead and take what they want." But he was not very sure. When he had something in his head he could easily put it forth, but when he was fallow there was nothing behind. Matisse often felt uncertain, but he never felt empty. He was eternally revolving the artist's eternal problem: how to realize (to use Cézanne's favorite term). This did not trouble Picasso. He had always been an illustrator, and when he had his theme he could easily develop it. . . .

His taste is impeccable (his fatal good taste, as someone has called it); he has a grace like that of Raphael, which is pervasive and perhaps his greatest real esthetic asset; he has humor, fancy, both light and tragic, invention, an abundant supply of qualities. He would have been a truly great artist, I think, if he had been more genuine; as it is, he's an extraordinary phenomenon. At the moment when I met him, he was at his best and made on me a strong impression. . . .

I saw Picasso often, either at the Rue Ravignan or the Rue de Fleurus. He was then in the last months of the Harlequin Period, painting acrobats and mountebanks. His inspiration had not yet run dry, for the best things of the period came then: *The Boy Leading a Horse,* and the large composition with a group of people, which I think was the last. With this period's end came an end to more than one of his characteristic periods; it was the end of an epoch in his life. It was Cézanne's fault, or rather the fault of Cézanne's reputation. Hitherto Cézanne had been important only for the few; he was about to become important for everybody. At the Autumn Salon of 1905 people laughed themselves into hysterics before his pictures, in 1906 they were respectful, and in 1907 they were reverent. Cézanne had become the man of the moment.

Matisse said once that Cézanne is "the father of us all," but he did not reckon with the phoenix Picasso, who had no father. Yet Cézanne could not be ignored. It was no longer a time for illustration, and Picasso for the first time tried for something that was not illustration at all: the result was deplorably feeble. This was the pink period, Picasso at his weakest. He did figures that were just figures, and there was hardly enough to them to make them worth doing. It was at this moment that I suggested he try working from the model in order to get more stuff into his figures. He came to my studio twice, but could make nothing of it; the few drawings he made did not, so to speak, look at the model. He also worked on Gertrude's portrait, but could not finish that.

Picasso's interior resources were too small for his then needs, and he had to have support from the outside. He found it in Negro art, which was a kind of substitute for an illustrative subject. With this he managed to "finish" Gertrude's portrait while we were away in Fiesole; though, as he left all except the mask as it had been before, the picture as a whole is incoherent. An artist, like a business man, needs a working capital; and if he can't make it by his own exertions, he has to borrow it. Picasso now borrowed it from the Negroes and it kept him going for a while. His forms grew bigger and in intention more powerful, but the reality was less than the appearance. I was not seriously interested in this stuff, but I was in his talent. Nor did I trust his morale. I often said that I had complete confidence in Matisse, who would give all that was possible for him to give, but that the future of Picasso was unpredictable, as there was no assured center. . . .

Matisse's work, unlike Picasso's, was one whose genuineness one could never question. He played with cubism a little and profited by Negro sculpture, but he was too intelligent and too sincere to drown in these things. He experimented, but kept control. One summer he brought back from the country a study of a young fisherman, and also a free copy of it with extreme deformations. At first he pretended that this had been made by the letter carrier of Collioure, but finally admitted that it was an experiment of his own. It was the first thing he did with forced deformations. He also brought back some landscapes in bright colors, which at first attracted me so strongly that I wanted the whole lot; but I could only get two of them, as the others were already promised. In these, for the first time, I noticed that after a little while the essential rhythm went flat. However, despite this, what he did always interested me, and I was always wanting to see what he did next. One could be certain that he was properly carrying on.

I thoroughly understood his work, and this he then recognized. One day he came to the house to ask me to do something. He was always diffident when asking, and it took some time for him to get to the point. Young men, office workers and others, had formed a group to visit the ateliers of painters, where someone would make a little speech about their work. He wanted me to make this speech for him. I declined. I said that I was ready to talk French extemporaneously, but not to address Frenchmen deliberately in their own tongue. Matisse urged me, as he said there was no one else to do it, but I had to refuse. I mention it as evidence from Matisse himself that I really understood him.

PORTRAITS
by Gertrude Stein

These portraits, written in 1909, were first published August 1912 by Alfred Stieglitz in a special number of *Camera Work,* his quarterly magazine devoted to photography and the activities of the Photo-Secession Gallery. They are reprinted here, by permission, from *Selected Writings of Gertrude Stein,* copyright 1946 by Random House, Inc.

HENRI MATISSE

ONE WAS quite certain that for a long part of his being one being living he had been trying to be certain that he was wrong in doing what he was doing and then when he could not come to be certain that he had been wrong in doing what he had been doing, when he had completely convinced himself that he would not come to be certain that he had been wrong in doing what he had been doing he was really certain then that he was a great one and he certainly was a great one. Certainly every one could be certain of this thing that this one is a great one.

Some said of him, when anybody believed in him they did not then believe in any other one. Certainly some said this of him.

He certainly very clearly expressed something. Some said that he did not clearly express anything. Some were certain that he expressed something very clearly and some of such of them said that he would have been a greater one if he had not been one so clearly expressing what he was expressing. Some said he was not clearly expressing what he was expressing and some of such of them said that the greatness of struggling which was not clear expression made of him one being a completely great one.

Some said of him that he was greatly expressing something struggling. Some said of him that he was not greatly expressing something struggling.

He certainly was clearly expressing something, certainly sometime any one might come to know that of him. Very many did come to know it of him that he was clearly expressing what he was expressing. He was a great one. Any one might come to know that of him. Very many did come to know that of him. Some who came to know that of him, that he was a great one, that he was clearly expressing something, came then to be certain that he was not greatly expressing something being struggling. Certainly he was expressing something being struggling. Any one could be certain that he was expressing something being struggling. Some were certain that he was greatly expressing this thing. Some were certain that he was not greatly expressing this thing. Every one could come to be certain that he was a great man. Any one could come to be certain that he was clearly expressing something.

Some certainly were wanting to be needing to be doing what he was doing, that is clearly expressing something. Certainly they were willing to be wanting to be a great one. They were, that is some of them, were not wanting to be needing expressing anything being struggling. And certainly he was one not greatly expressing something being struggling, he was a great one, he was clearly expressing something. Some were wanting to be doing what he was doing that is clearly expressing something. Very many were doing what he was doing, not greatly expressing something being struggling. Very many who were wanting to be doing what he was doing were not wanting to be expressing anything being struggling.

There were very many wanting to be doing what he was doing that is to be ones clearly expressing something. He was certainly a great man, any one could be really certain of this thing, every one could be certain of this thing. There were very many who were wanting to be ones doing what he was doing that is to be ones clearly expressing something and then very many of them were not wanting to be being ones doing that thing, that is clearly expressing something, they wanted to be ones expressing something being struggling, something being going to be some other thing, something being going to be something some one some-time would be clearly expressing and that would be something that would be a thing then that would then be greatly expressing some other thing than that thing, certainly very many were then not wanting to be doing what this one was doing clearly expressing something and some of them had been ones wanting to be doing that thing wanting to be ones clearly expressing something. Some were wanting to be ones doing what this one was doing wanted to be ones clearly expressing something. Some of such of them were ones certainly clearly expressing something, that was in them a thing not really interesting than any other one. Some of such of them went on being all their living ones wanting to be clearly expressing something and some of them were clearly expressing something.

This one was one very many were knowing some and very many were glad to meet him, very many sometimes listened to him, some listened to him very often, there were some who listened to him, and he talked then and he told them then that certainly he had been one suffering and he was then being one trying to be certain that he was wrong in doing what he was doing and he had come then to be certain that he never would be certain that he was doing what it was wrong for him to be doing then and he was suffering then and he was certain that he would be one doing what he was doing and he was certain that he should be one doing what he was doing and he was certain that he would always be one suffering and this then made him certain this, that he would always be one being suffering, this made him certain that he was expressing something being struggling and certainly very many were quite certain that he was greatly expressing something being struggling. This one was one knowing some who were listening to him and he was telling very often about being one suffering and this was not a dreary thing to any one hearing that then, it was not a saddening thing to any one hearing it again and again, to some

it was quite an interesting thing hearing it again and again, to some it was an exciting thing hearing it again and again, some knowing this one and being certain that this one was a great man and was one clearly expressing something were ones hearing this one telling about being one being living were hearing this one telling this thing again and again. Some who were ones knowing this one and were ones certain that this one was one who was clearly telling something, was a great man, were not listening very often to this one telling again and again about being one being living. Certainly some who were certain that this one was a great man and one clearly expressing something and greatly expressing something being struggling were listening to this one telling about being living telling about this again and again and again. Certainly very many knowing this one and being certain that this one was a great man and that this one was clearly telling something were not listening to this one telling about being living, were not listening to this one telling this again and again.

This one was certainly a great man, this one was certainly clearly expressing something. Some were certain that this one was clearly expressing something being struggling, some were certain that this one was not greatly expressing something being struggling.

Very many were not listening again and again to this one telling about being one being living. Some were listening again and again to this one telling about this one being one being in living.

Some were certainly wanting to be doing what this one was doing that is were wanting to be ones clearly expressing something. Some of such of them did not go on in being ones wanting to be doing what this one was doing that is in being ones clearly expressing something. Some went on being ones wanting to be doing what this one was doing that is, being ones clearly expressing something. Certainly this one was one who was a great man. Any one could be certain of this thing. Every one would come to be certain of this thing. This one was one certainly clearly expressing something. Any one could come to be certain of this thing. Every one would come to be certain of this thing. This one was one, some were quite certain, one greatly expressing something being struggling. This one was one, some were quite certain, one not greatly expressing something being struggling.

PABLO PICASSO

ONE WHOM some were certainly following was one who was completely charming. One whom some were certainly following was one who was charming. One whom some were following was one who was completely charming. One whom some were following was one who was certainly completely charming.

Some were certainly following and were certain that the one they were then following was one working and was one bringing out of himself then something. Some were certainly following and were certain that the one they were then following was one bringing out of himself then something that was coming to be a heavy thing, a solid thing and a complete thing.

One whom some were certainly following was one working and certainly was one bringing something out of himself then and was one who had been all his living had been one having something coming out of him.

Something had been coming out of him, certainly it had been coming out of him, certainly it was something, certainly it had been coming out of him and it had meaning, a charming meaning, a solid meaning, a struggling meaning, a clear meaning.

One whom some were certainly following and some were certainly following him, one whom some were certainly following was one certainly working.

One whom some were certainly following was one having something coming out of him something having meaning, and this one was certainly working then.

This one was working and something was coming then, something was coming out of this one then. This one was one and always there was something coming out of this one and always there had been something coming out of this one. This one had never been one not having something coming out of this one. This one was one having something coming out of this one. This one had been one whom some were following. This one was one whom some were following. This one was being one whom some were following. This one was one who was working.

This one was one who was working. This one was one being one having something being coming out of him. This one was one going on having something come out of him. This one was one going on working. This one was one whom some were following. This one was one who was working.

This one always had something being coming out of this one. This one was working. This one always had been working. This one was always having something that was coming out of this one that was a solid thing, a charming thing, a lovely thing, a perplexing thing, a disconcerting thing, a simple thing, a clear thing, a complicated thing, an interesting thing, a disturbing thing, a repellant thing, a very pretty thing. This one was one certainly being one having something coming out of him. This one was one whom some were following. This one was one who was working.

This one was one who was working and certainly this one was needing to be working so as to be one being working. This one was one having something coming out of him. This one would be one all his living having something coming out of him. This one was working and then this one was working and this one was needing to be working, not to be one having something coming out of him something having meaning, but was needing to be working so as to be one working.

This one was certainly working and working was something this one was certain this one would be doing and this one was doing that thing, this one was working. This one was not one completely working. This one was not ever completely working. This one certainly was not completely working.

This one was one having always something being coming out of him, something having completely a real meaning. This one was one whom some were following. This one was one who was working. This one was one who was working and he was one needing this thing needing to be working so as to be one having some way of being one having some way of working. This one was one who was working. This one was one having something come out of him something having meaning. This one was one always having something come out of him and this thing the thing coming out of him always had real meaning. This one was one who was working. This one was one who was almost always working. This one was not one completely working. This one was one not ever completely working. This one was not one working to have anything come out of him. This one did have something having meaning that did come out of him. He always did have something come out of him. He was working, he was not ever completely working. He did have some following. They were always following him. Some were certainly following him. He was one who was working. He was one having something coming out of him something having meaning. He was not ever completely working.

PLATE*S*

1 MATISSE. *Still Life with Chocolate Pot*. 1900.
Galerie Alex Maguy, Paris
2 *opposite* MATISSE. *View of Collioure*. 1908.
Collection Mr. and Mrs. Jacques Gelman, Mexico, D.F.

3 MATISSE. *Sideboard and Table*. 1899.
Dumbarton Oaks Collection, Washington, D.C.

4 MATISSE. *Olive Trees*. 1905.
Robert Lehman Collection, New York

5 MATISSE. *Landscape, Collioure*. 1905.
Collection Mr. and Mrs. David Rockefeller, New York

6 MATISSE. *Woman with a Branch of Ivy.* ca. 1905.
Collection Dr. and Mrs. Norman F. Laskey, Mt. Kisco, New York

To Elise from Sarah with love.   Henri Matisse

7 MATISSE. *Woman Leaning on Elbow*. 1906–7.
Collection Mr. and Mrs. Walter A. Haas, San Francisco

8 MATISSE. *Harbor at Collioure*. 1906? Lithograph.
The Museum of Modern Art, New York,
given anonymously in memory of Leo and Nina Stein

9 MATISSE. *André Derain*. 1905. The Tate Gallery, London
10 *opposite* MATISSE. *Margot*. 1907. Kunsthaus, Zurich

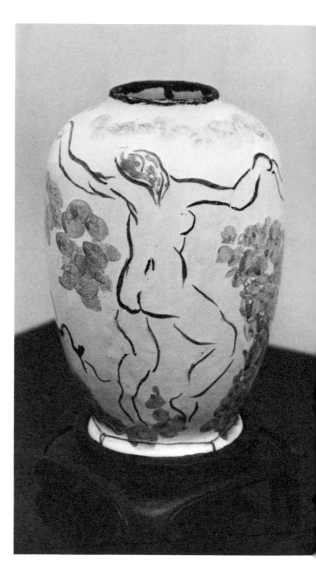

11 MATISSE. Ceramic Vase. ca. 1907.
Collection Mr. and Mrs. Lionel Steinberg, Palm Springs, California
12 *opposite* MATISSE. *Music (Study)*. 1907.
The Museum of Modern Art, New York,
gift of A. Conger Goodyear in honor of Alfred H. Barr, Jr.

Henri Matisse

13 *left* MATISSE. *The Serf.* 1900–1903.
The Museum of Modern Art, New York, Mr. and Mrs. Sam Salz Fund

14 *above* MATISSE. *Reclining Nude.* ca. 1908?
Collection Walter Stein, Port Washington, New York

15 MATISSE. *Nude before a Screen.* 1906.
Collection Robert Ardrey and Helen Johnson Ardrey,
Norman, Oklahoma

16 MATISSE. *Reclining Nude, I.* 1907.
The Museum of Modern Art, New York,
acquired through the Lillie P. Bliss Bequest

17 MATISSE. *The Blue Nude*. 1907.
The Baltimore Museum of Art, The Cone Collection

18 MATISSE. *Bronze with Carnations.* 1908.
Nasjonalgalleriet, Oslo

19 CÉZANNE. *Apples.* 1873–77.
Collection Eugene V. Thaw, New York

20 CÉZANNE. *Bathers*. ca. 1895.
The Baltimore Museum of Art, The Cone Collection

21 *left* MANET. *Ball Scene.* 1873.
Collection Johann Mustad, Göteborg, Sweden

22 *right* RENOIR. *Brunette.* 1890.
Collection Mr. and Mrs. Nelson R. Kandel, Baltimore

23 *opposite* BONNARD. *The Siesta.* 1900.
National Gallery of Victoria, Melbourne, Australia

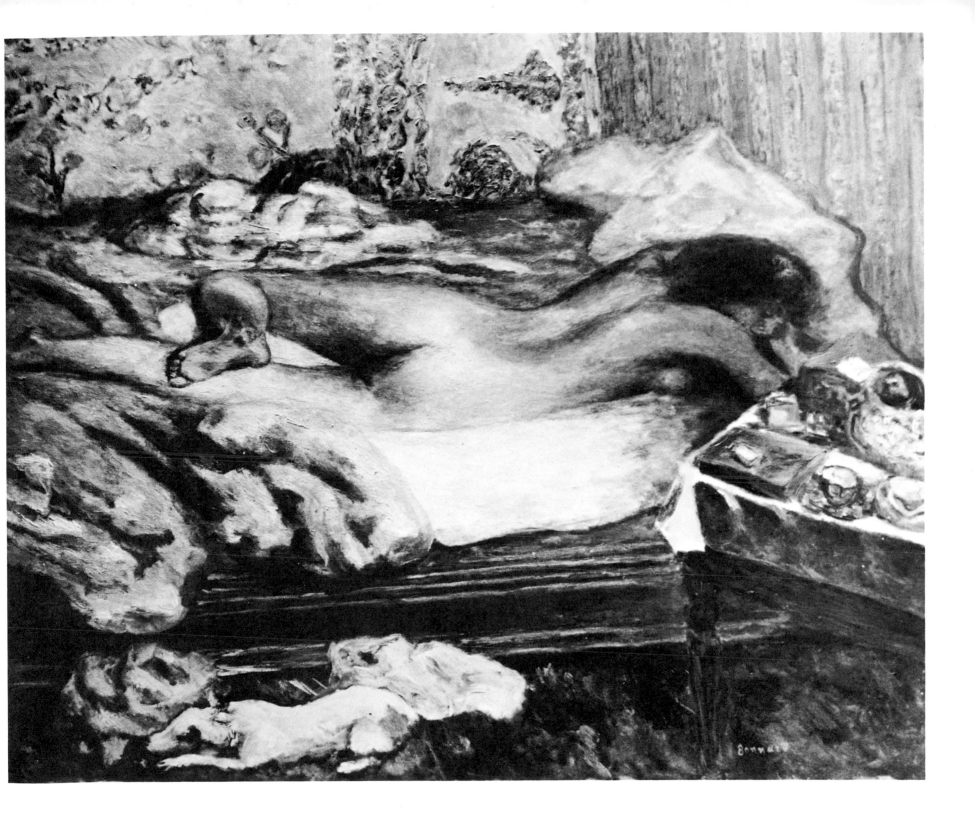

24 *opposite* GRIS. *Flowers.* 1914.
Private collection, New York

25 GRIS. *Dish of Pears.* 1926.
Collection Mr. and Mrs. David Rockefeller, New York

26 LAURENCIN. *Group of Artists*. 1908. The Baltimore Museum of Art, The Cone Collection.
(from left: Pablo Picasso, Fernande Olivier, Guillaume Apollinaire, Marie Laurencin)

27 *opposite* PICASSO. *Two Women at a Bar*. 1902.
Collection Walter P. Chrysler, Jr., New York

28 *opposite* PICASSO. *The Blue House.* 1902.
Collection André Meyer, New York

29 PICASSO. *Family Supper.* 1903.
Albright-Knox Art Gallery, Buffalo

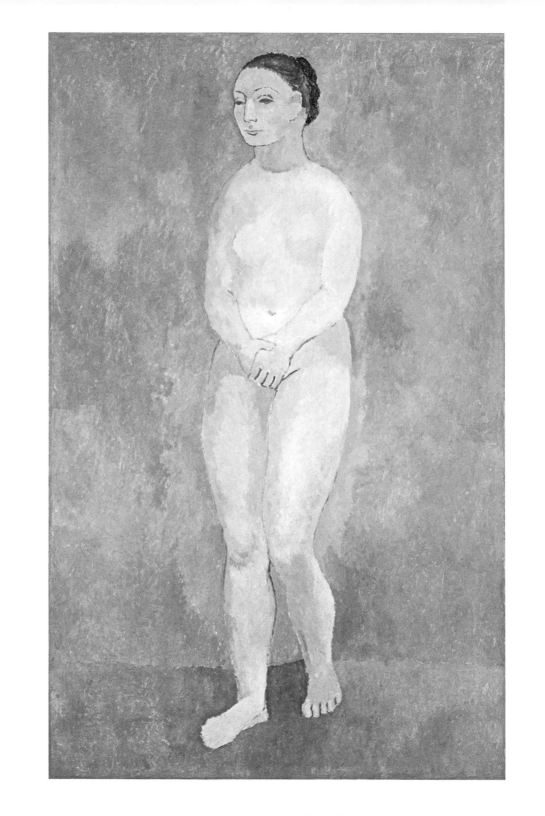

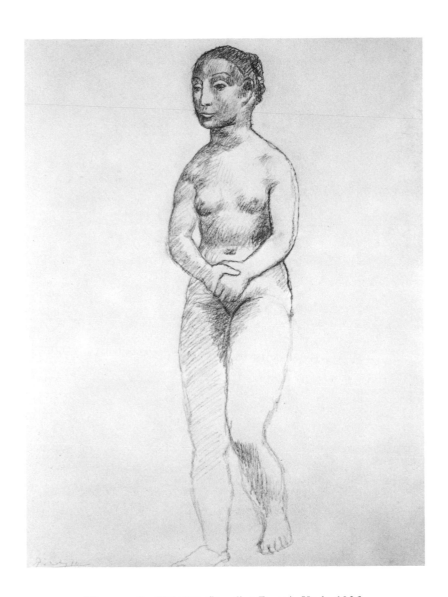

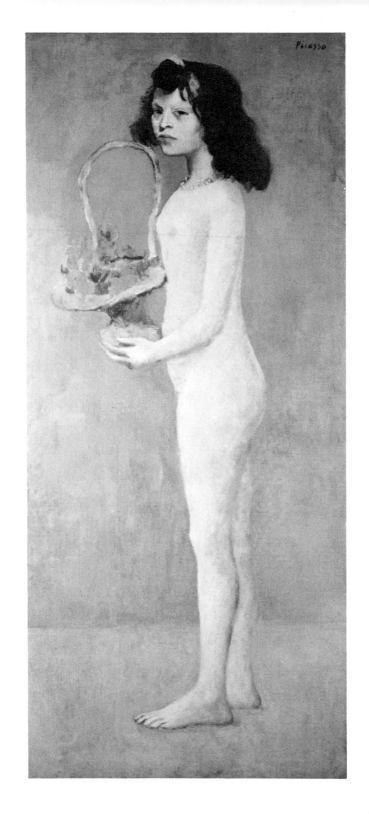

30 *opposite* PICASSO. *Standing Female Nude.* 1906.
Collection Mr. and Mrs. William S. Paley, New York

31 *above* PICASSO. *Standing Nude.* 1906.
Collection Mr. and Mrs. Leigh B. Block, Chicago

32 *right* PICASSO. *Young Girl with a Basket of Flowers.* 1905.
Collection Mr. and Mrs. David Rockefeller, New York

33 PICASSO. Sheet of Studies: *Self-Portrait and Nudes*. 1905.
Collection H. Arnold Steinberg, Montreal

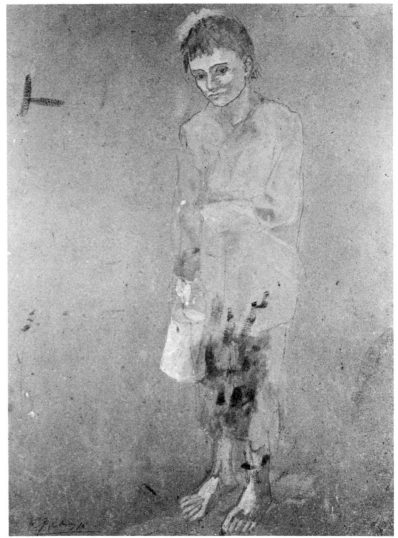

34 PICASSO. *Prodigal Son among Pigs.* 1906.
Collection Mr. and Mrs. Daniel Saidenberg, New York

35 PICASSO. *Boy with a Milk Can.* 1904.
Collection Mrs. Oveta Culp Hobby, Houston

36 *opposite* PICASSO. *Boy Leading a Horse*. 1905–6.
Collection Mr. and Mrs. William S. Paley, New York

37 PICASSO. *Woman with a Fan*. 1905.
Collection the Honorable and Mrs. W. Averell Harriman, Washington, D.C.

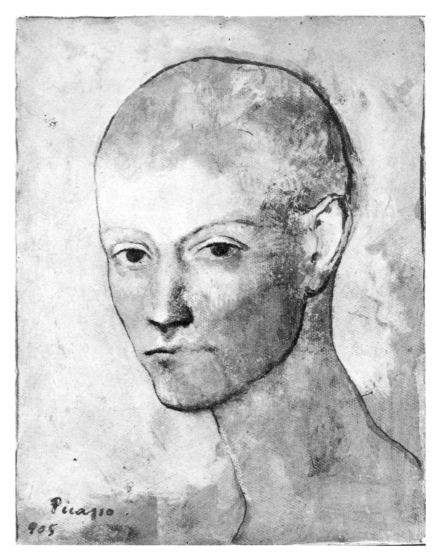

38 *left* PICASSO. *Head of a Man (Mask).* 1904–5.
The Baltimore Museum of Art, The Cone Collection

39 *right* PICASSO. *Head of a Boy.* 1905.
The Cleveland Museum of Art, bequest of Leonard C. Hanna, Jr.

40 *opposite* PICASSO. *The Acrobat's Family with a Monkey.* 1905.
Konstmuseum, Göteborg, Sweden

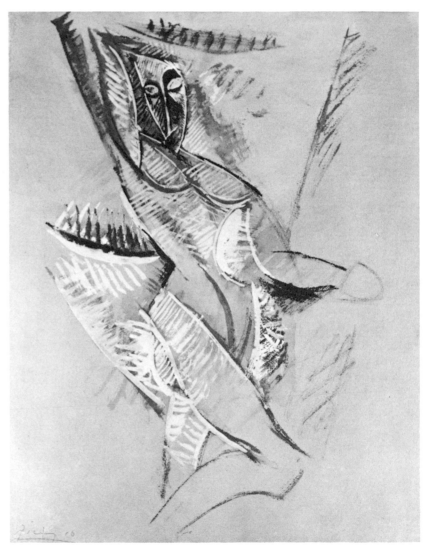

41 *left* PICASSO. Study for *Nude with Drapery*. 1907.
Collection Mr. and Mrs. John Hay Whitney, New York

42 *right* PICASSO. Study for *Nude with Drapery*. 1907.
Collection Mrs. Maurice L. Stone, New York

43 *opposite* PICASSO. *Nude with Drapery*. 1907. The Hermitage, Leningrad

44 PICASSO. *Still Life with Glasses and Fruit.* 1908.
Collection Nelson A. Rockefeller, New York

45 Picasso. *Still Life with Fruit and Glass.* 1908.
Collection Mr. and Mrs. John Hay Whitney, New York

7 PICASSO.
ase, Gourd, and
ruit on a Table. 1909.
ollection Mr. and Mrs.
ohn Hay Whitney,
ew York

48 PICASS
*Landscap
La Rue des Bois.* 190
Collection André Meye
New Yo

9 PICASSO.
*he Reservoir,
orta. 1909.
*ollection Mr. and Mrs.
*avid Rockefeller,
*ew York

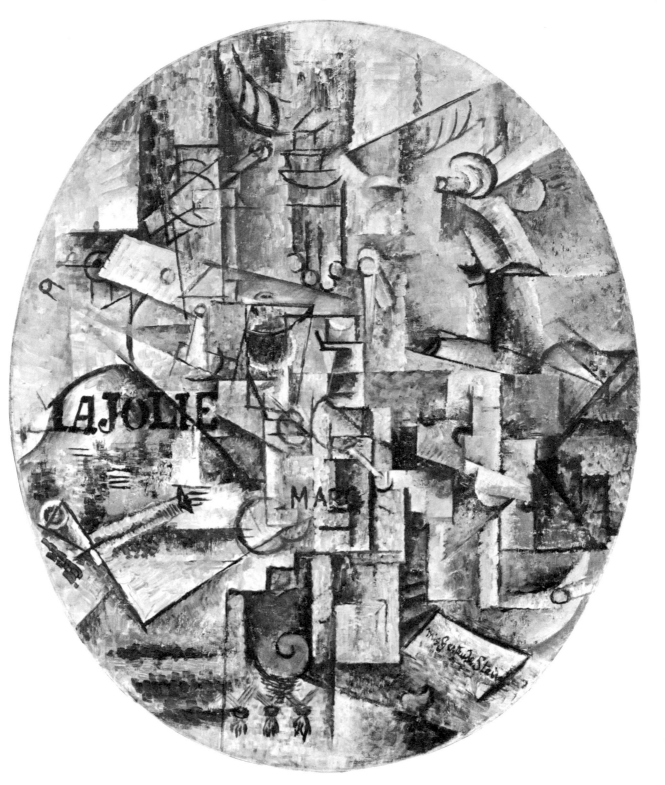

PICASSO.
Student with a Pipe.
1913–14. Collection
Nelson A. Rockefeller,
New York

52 *opposite* PICASSO. *Guitar on a Table*. 1912–13.
Collection Nelson A. Rockefeller, New York

53 *above* PICASSO. Study for *Guitar on a Table*. 1912–13.
Marlborough Gallery, Inc., New York

54 *right* PICASSO. *Woman with a Mandolin*. 1913–14.
Collection Mr. and Mrs. David Rockefeller, New York

55 *opposite* PICASSO. *Man with a Guitar.* 1913.
Collection André Meyer, New York

56 PICASSO. *Still Life with Fruit, Glass, Knife, and Newspaper.* 1914.
Collection Mr. and Mrs. David Lloyd Kreeger, Washington, D.C.

57 PICASSO. *Calligraphic Still Life.* 1922.
The Art Institute of Chicago, Ada Turnbull Hertle Fund

CATALOGUE OF THE EXHIBITION

Lenders

Robert Ardrey and Helen Johnson Ardrey; Leon Anthony Arkus; Dr. and Mrs. Harry Bakwin; George S. Block; Mr. and Mrs. Leigh B. Block; Mr. and Mrs. Gilbert W. Chapman; Walter P. Chrysler; Sidney E. and Roberta Cohn; Mrs. Andrew Cole; Mrs. J. H. Crang; Dominique Maurice-Denis; John W. Dodds; Alvin C. Eurich; Mr. and Mrs. Sampson R. Field; Mr. and Mrs. William A. Gaw; Mr. and Mrs. Jacques Gelman; Mr. and Mrs. Walter A. Haas; The Honorable and Mrs. W. Averell Harriman; Mrs. Oveta Culp Hobby; Mrs. Robert P. Hutchins; Mr. and Mrs. Tevis Jacobs; Riccardo Jucker; Mr. and Mrs. Nelson R. Kandel; Mr. and Mrs. David Lloyd Kreeger; Jan Krugier; Dr. and Mrs. Norman F. Laskey; Robert Lehman Collection; Mrs. Philip N. Lilienthal; Dr. and Mrs. Frederick H. Low; Jean Masurel; Pierre Matisse; Mr. and Mrs. Algur H. Meadows; André Meyer; Mr. and Mrs. Jan Mitchell; Johann Mustad; E. Jan Nadelman; Mr. and Mrs. William S. Paley; Henry Pearlman Foundation; Mr. and Mrs. Henry Pearlman; Picard Collection; Mr. and Mrs. Augustus Pollack; Lionel Prejger; Mr. and Mrs. Perry T. Rathbone; Mrs. Jerome B. Rocherolle; Mr. and Mrs. David Rockefeller; Nelson A. Rockefeller; Dr. and Mrs. Harold Rosenblum; Herbert and Nannette Rothschild; Mrs. Madeleine Haas Russell; Mr. and Mrs. Daniel Saidenberg; Mr. and Mrs. John D. Schiff; Mr. and Mrs. Georges E. Seligmann; Fred M. Stein Family; Walter Stein; H. Arnold Steinberg; Mr. and Mrs. Lionel Steinberg; Mrs. Maurice L. Stone; Eugene V. Thaw; Mr. and Mrs. Richard K. Weil; Mr. and Mrs. John Hay Whitney; Five anonymous lenders.

The Baltimore Museum of Art; Museum of Fine Arts, Boston; Albright-Knox Art Gallery, Buffalo; The Art Institute of Chicago; The Cleveland Museum of Art; Konstmuseum, Göteborg; The Museum of Fine Arts, Houston; The Hermitage, Leningrad; The Tate Gallery, London; National Gallery of Victoria, Melbourne; Collection of American Literature, Beinecke Rare Book and Manuscript Library, Yale University, New Haven; The Metropolitan Museum of Art, New York; The Museum of Modern Art, New York; Nasjonalgalleriet, Oslo; Musée du Louvre, Paris; Musée National d'Art Moderne, Paris; The Art Museum, Princeton University, Princeton, New Jersey; Museum of Art, Rhode Island School of Design, Providence; Brigham Young University Art Collection, Provo, Utah; San Francisco Museum of Art; Dumbarton Oaks Collection, Washington, D.C.; Kunsthaus, Zurich.

Wally F. Findlay Galleries International, Inc., Chicago; Marlborough Gallery, Inc., New York; Galerie Alex Maguy, Paris.

Catalogue

The catalogue is arranged alphabetically by artist, with the works of each artist arranged chronologically, and works of the same year listed alphabetically by title. A date enclosed in parentheses does not appear on the work itself. In dimensions, height precedes width. The name of the member of the Stein family who first owned each work is given in parentheses, preceding the name of the present owner. In the case of prints and sculpture, it is not known in every instance whether the impression or cast in the exhibition is the one actually owned by the Steins.

Several entries include quotations from the writings of Gertrude or Leo Stein or comments by the director of the exhibition. Quotations appear in italic, comments in roman type. The sources of the quotations are: [Gertrude Stein], *The Autobiography of Alice B. Toklas,* New York: Harcourt, Brace and Company, 1933; Gertrude Stein, *Picasso,* Boston: Beacon Press, 1959 (originally published in French, Paris: Librairie Floury, 1938); Leo Stein, *Appreciation: Painting, Poetry and Prose,* New York: Crown Publishers, 1947; [Leo Stein], *Journey into the Self: Being the Letters, Papers & Journals of Leo Stein,* edited by Edmund Fuller, New York: Crown Publishers, 1950.

CHRISTIAN BÉRARD. 1902–1949

Gertrude Stein. 1928. Ink on paper, 13½ x 10½". (Gertrude Stein). Collection of American Literature, Beinecke Rare Book and Manuscript Library, Yale University, New Haven.

EUGENE BERMAN. born 1899

Portrait of Alice B. Toklas. (ca. 1930). India ink on paper, 22 x 17". (Alice B. Toklas). Collection Gilbert A. Harrison, Washington, D.C.

PIERRE BONNARD. 1867–1947

The Siesta. (1900). Oil on canvas, 43 x 51½". (Leo and Gertrude Stein). National Gallery of Victoria, Melbourne, Australia. *Plate 23.*

PAUL CÉZANNE, 1839–1906

Apples. (1873–77). Oil on canvas, 4⅞ x 10¼". (Leo and Gertrude Stein). Collection Eugene V. Thaw, New York. *Plate 19.*
The Cézanne apples have a unique importance to me that nothing can replace...The Cézannes had to be divided. I am willing to leave you the Picasso oeuvre, as you left me the Renoir, and you can have everything except that I want to keep the few drawings that I have...and I'm afraid you'll have to look upon the loss of the apples as an act of God.— Letter from Leo to Gertrude Stein (1913–14?), Journey into the Self, p. 57.

Portrait of the Artist's Son, Paul. (1880). Oil on canvas, 6¾ x 6". (Michael and Sarah Stein). Collection Mr. and Mrs. Henry Pearlman, New York.

Environs de Gardanne. (1885–86). Watercolor on paper, 12¼ x 18¾". (Leo and Gertrude Stein). Private collection, New York.

Bathers in Landscape. (ca. 1890–97). Lithograph, printed in color, 9⅜ x 12⅝". (Leo and Gertrude Stein; Michael and Sarah Stein). The Museum of Modern Art, New York, gift of Abby Aldrich Rockefeller.

Bathers. (ca. 1895). Oil on canvas, 10⅝ x 18⅛". (Leo and Gertrude Stein). The Baltimore Museum of Art, The Cone Collection. *Plate 20.*

Bathers. (1899). Lithograph, printed in color, 16¾ x 20⅝".

(Leo and Gertrude Stein). The Museum of Modern Art, New York, Lillie P. Bliss Collection.

Mont Ste.-Victoire (ca. 1900). Watercolor on paper, 12¼ x 18¾". (Leo and Gertrude Stein). Musée du Louvre, Paris.

OTHON COUBINE. 1883–1969

Orchard with Purple Heather. (mid-1920s?). Oil on canvas, 23½ x 28½". (Leo Stein). Collection Fred M. Stein Family, New York.

HONORÉ DAUMIER. 1808–1879

Head of an Old Woman. (1856–60). Oil on panel, 8⅝ x 6½". (Leo and Gertrude Stein). Henry Pearlman Foundation, New York.
They had soon the privilege of upsetting his [Vollard's] piles of canvases and finding what they liked in the heap. They bought a tiny little Daumier, head of an old woman.—Gertrude Stein, Autobiography of Alice B. Toklas, p. 38.

JO DAVIDSON, 1883–1952

Gertrude Stein. (ca. 1923). Bronze (recast, 1949, from mold used to reproduce a miniature version in pewter of the almost life-size original), 7¾" high. (Gertrude Stein). Collection of American Literature, Beinecke Rare Book and Manuscript Library, Yale University, New Haven.
Jo Davidson too sculptured Gertrude Stein at this time. There, all was peaceful, Jo was witty and amusing and he pleased Gertrude Stein.—Gertrude Stein, Autobiography of Alice B. Toklas, p. 251.

Bilignin. (ca. 1930). Watercolor on paper, 7⅝ x 11¼". (Gertrude Stein). Collection of American Literature, Beinecke Rare Book and Manuscript Library, Yale University, New Haven.

DAUMIER. *Head of an Old Woman.* 1856–60.
Henry Pearlman Foundation, New York

MAURICE DENIS. 1870–1943

Mother in Black. 1895. Oil on canvas, 18⅛ x 15". (Leo and Gertrude Stein). Collection Dominique Maurice-Denis, Saint-Germain-en-Laye.

JUAN GRIS. 1887–1927

Glass and Bottle. (1913–14). Oil and pasted paper on canvas, 24⅛ x 15⅛". (Gertrude Stein). Collection André Meyer, New York.

Book and Glasses. (1914). Oil, pasted paper, and crayon on canvas, 25¾ x 19¾". (Gertrude Stein). Private collection, New York.

Flowers. (1914). Oil, pasted paper, and pencil on canvas, 21¾ x 18¼". (Gertrude Stein). Private collection, New York. *Plate 24.*

The Table in Front of the Window. 1921. Oil on canvas, 25⅝ x 39½". (Gertrude Stein). Private collection, New York.

The Clown. 1924. Ink on paper, 9⅞ x 7½". Inscribed: "A Gertrude Stein/tres amicalement/Juan Gris/1924." (Gertrude Stein). Collection Mr. and Mrs. Lionel Steinberg, Palm Springs, California. *Page 69.*

Seated Woman. 1924. Oil on canvas, 32 x 23⅝". (Gertrude Stein). Private collection, New York.

Study: *Ship's Deck (Boat Deck).* (1924). Watercolor and pasted paper on paper 8½ x 11¾". Inscribed: "A Gertrude Stein/son ami Juan Gris 1925." (Gertrude Stein). Collection Nelson A. Rockefeller, New York. *Page 71.*

The Green Cloth. 1925. Oil on canvas, 28¾ x 36¼". (Gertrude Stein). Collection Mr. and Mrs. David Rockefeller, New York.

A Book Concluding with As a Wife Has a Cow. (1926). Four lithographs, each 9½ x 7⅜" (sheet size). (Gertrude Stein). The Museum of Modern Art, New York, gift of James Thrall Soby.
These lithographs were commissioned as illustrations for a text by Gertrude Stein, published by D.-H. Kahnweiler in 1926.

Dish of Pears. 1926. Oil on canvas, 10⅝ x 13¾". (Gertrude Stein). Collection Mr. and Mrs. David Rockefeller, New York. *Plate 25.*

MARIE LAURENCIN. 1885–1956

Group of Artists. 1908. Oil on canvas, 24¾ x 31⅛". (Leo and Gertrude Stein). The Baltimore Museum of Art, The Cone Collection. *Plate 26.*
In the early days Marie Laurencin painted a strange picture, portraits of Guillaume [Apollinaire], Picasso, Fernande and herself. Fernande told Gertrude Stein about it. Gertrude Stein bought it and Marie Laurencin was so pleased. It was the first picture of hers any one had ever bought.—Gertrude Stein, Autobiography of Alice B. Toklas, pp. 76–77.

JACQUES LIPCHITZ. born 1891

Gertrude Stein. (1920). Bronze, 13⅜". (Gertrude Stein). The Museum of Modern Art, New York, gift of friends of the artist.
He had just finished a bust of Jean Cocteau and he wanted to do her. She never minds posing, she likes the calm of it and although she does not like sculpture and told Lipchitz so, she began to pose. I remember it was a very hot spring and Lipchitz's studio was appallingly hot and they spent hours there.
Lipchitz is an excellent gossip and Gertrude Stein adores

the beginning and middle and end of a story and Lipchitz was able to supply several missing parts of several stories.

And then they talked about art and Gertrude Stein rather liked her portrait and they were very good friends and the sittings were over.—Gertrude Stein, Autobiography of Alice B. Toklas, p. 249.

ÉDOUARD MANET. 1832–1883

Ball Scene. (1873). Oil on canvas, 13¾ x 10⅝". (Leo and Gertrude Stein). Collection Johan Mustad, Göteborg, Sweden. *Plate 21.*
We had an exquisite little Manet.—Leo Stein, Appreciation: Painting, Poetry and Prose, p. 198.
They found a very very small Manet painted in black and white with Forain in the foreground and bought it.—Gertrude Stein, Autobiography of Alice B. Toklas, p. 38.

HENRI MANGUIN. 1874–1949

Standing Nude. (ca. 1904–5). Oil on canvas, 24¾ x 21". (Leo and Gertrude Stein). Private collection, New York. *The following spring [1905] I went through the Independents' as thoroughly as I had gone through the Autumn Salon …I bought…a successful study of the nude by Manguin, really school of Matisse, but of a kind of Matisse that I had not yet seen; otherwise I should not have been so well pleased with this Matisse at second-hand.*—Leo Stein, Appreciation: Painting, Poetry and Prose, p. 158.

LOUIS MARCOUSSIS. 1883–1941

Gertrude Stein. (ca. 1933). Engraving, 14 x 11". (Gertrude Stein). The Museum of Modern Art, New York, gift of Victor S. Riesenfeld.

LIPCHITZ. *Gertrude Stein.* 1920
The Museum of Modern Art, New York,
gift of friends of the artist

ANDRÉ MASSON. born 1896

The Cardplayers. (1923). Oil on canvas, 31⅞ x 23⅝".
(Gertrude Stein). Private collection, Paris.
*The next painter who attracted her attention was André
Masson. Masson was at that time influenced by Juan Gris
in whom Gertrude Stein's interest was permanent and vital.
She was interested in André Masson as a painter particu-
larly as a painter of white and she was interested in his com-
position in the wandering line in his compositions.*—Gertrude
Stein, Autobiography of Alice B. Toklas, p. 258.

HENRI MATISSE. 1869–1954

The Open Door. Brittany, Summer 1896. Oil on canvas,
13½ x 11" (sight). (Michael and Sarah Stein). Private
collection.

Ajaccio. Corsica (1898). Oil on canvas, 11 x 14¼". (Michael
and Sarah Stein). Collection Mrs. Philip N. Lilienthal, Burlingame, California.

The Canal of the Midi. Toulouse (Winter 1898–99). Oil on
canvas, 9½ x 14½". (Michael and Sarah Stein). Collection
Mr. and Mrs. Lionel Steinberg, Palm Springs, California.

Still Life. (1899). Pencil on paper, 4⅝ x 5¼". (Michael
and Sarah Stein). The Baltimore Museum of Art, The Cone
Collection.

The Invalid. Toulouse (early 1899). Oil on canvas, 18⅛
x 15". (Leo and Gertrude Stein). The Baltimore Museum
of Art, The Cone Collection.

Sideboard and Table. Toulouse (early 1899). Oil on canvas,
26½ x 32½". (Michael and Sarah Stein). Dumbarton Oaks
Collection, Washington, D.C. *Plate 3.*

Male Nude. (ca. 1900). Oil on canvas, 32¼ x 11½". (Michael and Sarah Stein). Private collection, San Francisco.

Still Life with Chocolate Pot. Paris (1900). Oil on canvas,
28¾ x 23½". (Michael and Sarah Stein). Galerie Alex
Maguy, Paris. *Plate 1.*

The Serf. Paris (1900–1903). Bronze, 37⅜" high. (Leo
and Gertrude Stein; Michael and Sarah Stein). The Museum of Modern Art, New York, Mr. and Mrs. Sam Salz
Fund. *Plate 13.*
*Matisse spent three years and more than a hundred sittings
on a small statue, which at the end looked to the average
person as though it might have been done in an afternoon
... I had seen this figure in plaster several times and admired
it, but it was only when I saw it in bronze that my enthusiasm flamed, and I bought it.*—Leo Stein, Appreciation:
Painting, Poetry and Prose, p. 33.

Madeleine, I. (1901). Bronze, 23⅝" high. (Michael and
Sarah Stein). The Baltimore Museum of Art, The Cone
Collection.

Woman with Black Hair. (ca. 1902). Oil on canvas, 17½ x
14½". (Michael and Sarah Stein). Collection Mrs. Andrew
Cole, San Francisco.

André Derain. (1905). Oil on canvas, 15½ x 11⅜". (Michael and Sarah Stein). The Tate Gallery, London. *Plate 9.*

Japanese Woman beside the Water. Collioure (1905). Oil
on canvas, 13¾ x 11". (Michael and Sarah Stein). Collection Mrs. Philip N. Lilienthal, Burlingame, California.

Landscape, Collioure. (1905). Oil on panel, 18 x 21¾".
(Michael and Sarah Stein). Collection Mr. and Mrs. David
Rockefeller, New York. *Plate 5.*

Landscape, Les Genêts. (1905). Oil on canvas, 12¾ x 16".
(Michael and Sarah Stein). Collection Mr. and Mrs. Walter
A. Haas, San Francisco.

Madame Matisse in Garden. (1905). Ink on paper, 8 x

10½". (Michael and Sarah Stein). Collection Mr. and Mrs. Lionel Steinberg, Palm Springs, California.

Olive Trees. (1905). Oil on canvas, 18⅛ x 21⅝". (Leo and Gertrude Stein). Robert Lehman Collection, New York. *Plate 4*.

Portrait of Pierre Matisse. (1905). Bronze, 6⅛" high. (Michael and Sarah Stein). The Baltimore Museum of Art, The Cone Collection.

Seascape (Bord de mer). Collioure (1905). Oil on wood, 9⅜ x 12¼". (Michael and Sarah Stein). San Francisco Museum of Art, Mildred B. Bliss Bequest.

Seascape (Marine). Collioure (1905). Oil on wood, 9⅜ x 12¼". (Michael and Sarah Stein). San Francisco Museum of Art, Mildred B. Bliss Bequest.

Woman Leaning on Her Hands. (1905). Bronze, 5¼" high. (Michael and Sarah Stein). The Baltimore Museum of Art, The Cone Collection.

Woman with a Branch of Ivy (L'Italienne). (ca. 1905). Oil on canvas, 15¾ x 12½". (Michael and Sarah Stein). Collection Dr. and Mrs. Norman F. Laskey, Mt. Kisco, New York. *Plate 6*.

Figure in a Landscape. Collioure (1905–6). Watercolor on paper, 7 x 10". (Michael and Sarah Stein). Collection Mr. and Mrs. Tevis Jacobs, San Francisco.

Harbor at Collioure. Collioure (1906?). Lithograph, 4⅜ x 7⅝". Inscribed: "hommage à Mademoiselle Stein/Henri-Matisse." (Gertrude Stein). The Museum of Modern Art, New York, given anonymously in memory of Leo and Nina Stein. *Plate 8*.

Head of a Young Girl. (1906). Bronze, 6½" high. (Michael and Sarah Stein). The Baltimore Museum of Art, The Cone Collection.

Head of a Young Girl with Upswept Hair. (1906). Bronze, 4¼" high. (Michael and Sarah Stein). Collection Dr. and Mrs. Harry Bakwin, New York.

Madame Matisse Pinning Her Hat. (ca. 1906). Ink on paper, 11⅝ x 7⅝". (Gertrude Stein). Collection of American Literature, Beinecke Rare Book and Manuscript Library, Yale University, New Haven.
Gertrude Stein always liked the way she pinned her hat to her head and Matisse once made a drawing of his wife making this characteristic gesture and gave it to Miss Stein. She always wore black. She always placed a large black hat-pin well in the middle of the hat and the middle of the top of her head and then with a large firm gesture, down it came.— Gertrude Stein, Autobiography of Alice B. Toklas, pp. 43–44.

Nude before a Screen. (1906). Oil on canvas, 13 x 7½". (Michael and Sarah Stein). Collection Robert Ardrey and Helen Johnson Ardrey, Norman, Oklahoma. *Plate 15*.
Sarah and Michael Stein returned to San Francisco in the spring of 1906 to inspect their property after the disastrous earthquake and fire. They brought with them three small paintings and a drawing by Matisse, the first works of the artist to be seen in America. Among them was this painting.

Nude in Landscape. Collioure (1906). Oil on panel, 15¾ x 12⅝". (Michael and Sarah Stein). Wally F. Findlay Galleries International, Inc., Chicago.

Nude Seated in a Folding Chair. (1906). Lithograph, 14¾ x 10⅝". (Leo and Gertrude Stein). The Museum of Modern Art, New York, given anonymously in memory of Leo and Nina Stein.

Sailboat in the Harbor of Collioure. (1906?). Brush and ink on paper, 6 x 8" (sight). Inscribed on mount: "A Allain Stein/son ami H. Matisse 7 nov. 07." (Allan Stein). Private collection.

Sketch for *Marguerite Reading*. (1906). Oil on canvas, 5¼

x 5½". (Michael and Sarah Stein). Collection Pierre Matisse, New York.

Small Head. (1906). Bronze, 3⅜" high. (Michael and Sarah Stein). The Baltimore Museum of Art, The Cone Collection.

Standing Nude Reading. (1906?). Lithograph, 24 x 18". (Michael and Sarah Stein). Collection Mr. and Mrs. William A. Gaw, Berkeley, California.

Woman and Still Life. (1906?). Oil on canvas, 12½ x 15¾". (Michael and Sarah Stein). Private collection, San Francisco.

Yellow Pottery from Provence (The Yellow Jug). Collioure (1906). Oil on canvas, 21¼ x 17¾". (Leo and Gertrude Stein). The Baltimore Museum of Art, The Cone Collection.

Reclining Nude. Collioure (Summer 1906). Oil on canvas, 12¾ x 15½". (Michael and Sarah Stein). Collection Mrs. Madeleine Haas Russell, San Francisco.

Sketch: *The Artist's Family.* July 4, 1906. Ink on paper (postcard), 3¼ x 4¼". (Michael and Sarah Stein). Private collection, San Francisco.

Woman Leaning on Elbow. (1906–7?). Ink on paper, 10½ x 8½". Inscribed (at a later date): "To Elise [Haas] from Sarah with love." (Michael and Sarah Stein). Collection Mr. and Mrs. Walter A. Haas, San Francisco. *Plate 7.*

Ceramic Vase. (ca. 1907). Ceramic, painted, 9¼" high. (Michael and Sarah Stein). Collection Mr. and Mrs. Lionel Steinberg, Palm Springs, California. *Plate 11.*

Dancing Faun. (1907?). Ceramic tile, 5 x 4¾". (Michael and Sarah Stein). Collection John W. Dodds, Stanford, California.

Margot (Marguerite in a Veiled Hat). (1907). Oil on canvas, 31⅞ x 25⅝". (Leo and Gertrude Stein). Kunsthaus, Zurich. *Plate 10.*

Reclining Nude, I. Collioure (1907). Bronze, 13½" high x 19¾" long. (Michael and Sarah Stein). The Museum of Modern Art, New York, acquired through the Lillie P. Bliss Bequest. *Plate 16.*

Studies of Allan Stein. 1907. Brush and ink on paper, 21½ x 17½". Inscribed: "A Allan Stein/en souvenir de les onze ans/affectueusement/mai 1907 Henri Matisse." (Allan Stein). Private collection.

The Blue Nude (Souvenir of Biskra). Collioure (early 1907). Oil on canvas, 36¼ x 55⅛". (Gertrude and Leo Stein). The Baltimore Museum of Art, The Cone Collection. *Plate 17.*

During the three years that followed on the Woman with the Hat *I bought a number of Matisses—the last one,* The Blue Woman, *now in the Cone collection in Baltimore, but really a pink woman in blue scenery.—Leo Stein, Appreciation: Painting, Poetry and Prose, p. 162.*

Then we went on and saw a Matisse. Ah there we were beginning to feel at home. We knew a Matisse when we saw it, knew at once and enjoyed it and knew that it was great art and beautiful. It was a big figure of a woman lying in among some cactuses. A picture which was after the show [Indépendants, 1907] to be at the rue de Fleurus.—Gertrude Stein, Autobiography of Alice B. Toklas, p. 21.

Leo Stein lent this work to the Armory Show in 1913.

Music (Study). Collioure (Summer 1907). Oil on canvas, 29 x 24". (Leo and Gertrude Stein). The Museum of Modern Art, New York, gift of A. Conger Goodyear in honor of Alfred H. Barr, Jr. *Plate 12.*

Sketch for Ceramic Design. (ca. 1907–9). Pencil on paper, 4 x 5⅝". (Michael and Sarah Stein). San Francisco Museum of Art, gift of Charles Lindstrom.

Bronze with Carnations. (1908). Oil on canvas, 23⅝ x 29". (Michael and Sarah Stein). Nasjonalgalleriet, Oslo. *Plate 18.*

Pig. (ca. 1908). Pencil on paper, 8 x 12" (sight). (Michael and Sarah Stein). Private collection.

Reclining Nude. (ca. 1908?). Ink on paper, 8 x 9". (Michael and Sarah Stein). Collection Walter Stein, Port Washington, New York. *Plate 14.*

Small Crouching Nude without an Arm. (1908?). Bronze, 5¾" high. (Michael and Sarah Stein). Collection Mr. and Mrs. Lionel Steinberg, Palm Springs, California.
Sarah Stein told the present owners of this bronze that Matisse picked her up at their school in Paris for a walk in the rain, and drew this sculpture from his raincoat pocket, breaking off the arm. He was greatly disturbed and wanted to destroy it, but she persuaded him not to, and he cast it that way.

Two Negresses. (1908). Bronze, 18½" high. (Michael and Sarah Stein). The Baltimore Museum of Art, The Cone Collection.

View of Collioure. Collioure (1908). Oil on canvas, 35¾ x 24¾". (Michael and Sarah Stein). Collection Mr. and Mrs. Jacques Gelman, Mexico, D.F. *Plate 2.*

Sarah Stein. (1908–11?). Oil on canvas, 25 x 19¼" (sight). (Michael and Sarah Stein). Private collection.

Nude in Forest. Cavalière (Summer 1909). Oil on canvas, 16½ x 13". (Michael and Sarah Stein). Collection Mr. and Mrs. Tevis Jacobs, San Francisco.

Three Studies of Marguerite. (1910?). Ink on paper, 10 x 15½". (Michael and Sarah Stein). Collection Mr. and Mrs. Walter A. Haas, San Francisco.

Collioure. (1911). Oil on canvas, 24¾ x 20⅛". (Michael and Sarah Stein). Collection Nelson A. Rockefeller, New York.

Portrait of Claribel Cone. (1913). Pencil on paper, 10¾ x 8" (sight). (Michael and Sarah Stein). Private collection.

MATISSE. *Small Crouching Nude without an Arm.* 1908?
Collection Mr. and Mrs. Lionel Steinberg,
Palm Springs, California

Portrait of Etta Cone. (1913). Pencil on paper, 10½ x 8″ (sight). (Michael and Sarah Stein). Private Collection.

Untitled. (1913). Ink on paper, 11 x 8″. (Michael and Sarah Stein). Collection Alvin C. Eurich, New York.

Black Eyes. (1914). Lithograph, 17⅞ x 12¾″. (Michael and Sarah Stein). The Museum of Modern Art, New York, gift of Mrs. Saidie A. May.

Figure. (ca. 1914). Monotype, 4¼ x 2½″. (Michael and Sarah Stein). Collection George S. Block, San Francisco.

Head. (1914?). Drypoint, 10¾ x 8″ (sight). (Michael and Sarah Stein). Collection Mr. and Mrs. William A. Gaw, Berkeley, California.

Irène Vignier. (1914). Monotype, 6⅛ x 2¼″. (Michael and Sarah Stein). Collection Mr. and Mrs. Lionel Steinberg, Palm Springs, California.

Nude with Face Half-Hidden. (1914). Lithograph, 19¾ x 12″. (Michael and Sarah Stein). The Museum of Modern Art, New York, Frank Crowninshield Fund.

Seated Nude. (1914). Drypoint etching, 5¾ x 4″. (Michael and Sarah Stein). The Museum of Modern Art, New York.

Seated Nude, Back Turned. (1914). Lithograph, 16⅝ x 10⅜″. (Michael and Sarah Stein). Collection Mrs. Philip N. Lilienthal, Burlingame, California.

Portrait of Michael Stein. Paris, 1916. Oil on canvas, 26½ x 19⅞″. (Michael and Sarah Stein). San Francisco Museum of Art, gift of Nathan Cummings to the Sarah and Michael Stein Memorial Collection. *Page 34.*

Study for *Portrait of Sarah Stein.* Paris, 1916. Charcoal on paper, 19⅜ x 12⅝″. Inscribed: "à Madᵉ Michel Stein/ hommage respectueux/Henri-Matisse 1916." (Sarah Stein). San Francisco Museum of Art, gift of Mr. and Mrs. Walter A. Haas.

Portrait of Sarah Stein. Paris, 1916. Oil on canvas, 28⅝ x 22¼″. (Michael and Sarah Stein). San Francisco Museum of Art, gift of Mr. and Mrs. Walter A. Haas to the Sarah and Michael Stein Memorial Collection. *Page 34.*

The Organdy Dress. (1922). Lithograph, 16¾ x 10⅞″. (Michael and Sarah Stein). The Museum of Modern Art, New York, gift of Abby Aldrich Rockefeller.

Seated Girl in Garden. (1922). Lithograph, 16⅛ x 20⅜″. Inscribed: "à M. et Mme. Michel Stein — cordialement." (Michael and Sarah Stein). Collection Mr. and Mrs. Tevis Jacobs, San Francisco.

Arabesque. (1924). Lithograph, 19⅛ x 12⅝″. (Michael and Sarah Stein). The Museum of Modern Art, New York, Lillie P. Bliss Collection.

Portrait of Mrs. Allan Stein. (1924). Charcoal on paper, 25 x 19″. Inscribed: "aux epoux Allan Stein Daunt/souvenir amical/Henri Matisse/24." (Allan Stein). Collection Mr. and Mrs. Lionel Steinberg, Palm Springs, California.

Odalisque. (1925). Lithograph, 20 x 16″. (Michael and Sarah Stein). Collection Mrs. Philip N. Lilienthal, Burlingame, California.

Seated Woman. (1925). Lithograph, 13 x 10″. (Michael and Sarah Stein). Collection Mr. and Mrs. Tevis Jacobs, San Francisco.

Nude. n.d. Pencil on paper, 11 x 9″. (Michael and Sarah Stein). Collection Dr. and Mrs. Harold Rosenblum, Sausalito, California.

CHARLES MERYON. 1821–1868

The Morgue. 1854. Etching, 8¾ x 7¾″ (clipped). (Leo and Gertrude Stein). The Metropolitan Museum of Art, New York, bequest of Susan Dwight Bliss, 1967.

ELIE NADELMAN. 1882–1946

Standing Woman. (1907; cast ca. 1926). Bronze, 30″ high. (Leo and Gertrude Stein). Collection E. Jan Nadelman, Washington, D.C.

FRANCIS PICABIA. 1878–1953

Gertrude Stein. (early 1930s). Oil on canvas, 29½ x 24″ (sight). (Gertrude Stein). Private collection.
She is interested in Picabia in whom hitherto she has never been interested because he at least knows that if you do not solve your painting problem in painting human beings you do not solve it at all.—Gertrude Stein, Autobiography of Alice B. Toklas, p. 146.

PABLO PICASSO. born 1881

Café Scene. Paris (1900). Oil on canvas, 10 x 13¼″. (Alice B. Toklas). Collection of American Literature, Beinecke Rare Book and Manuscript Library, Yale University, New Haven.
Once about this time Picasso looking at this [Le Divan by Toulouse-Lautrec] and greatly daring said, but all the same I do paint better than he did. Toulouse-Lautrec had been the most important of his early influences. I later bought a little tiny picture by Picasso of that epoch.—Gertrude Stein, Autobiography of Alice B. Toklas, p. 12.

The Blue House. Barcelona (1902). Oil on canvas, 20⅜ x 16⅜″. (Leo and Gertrude Stein). Collection André Meyer, New York. *Plate 28.*

Head of a Bearded Man. Barcelona (1902). Charcoal on paper, 12 x 8½″. (Leo and Gertrude Stein). Collection Leon Anthony Arkus, Pittsburgh.

Soup. Barcelona (1902). Oil on canvas, 14½ x 17¾″. (Michael and Sarah Stein). Collection Mrs. J. H. Crang, Toronto.

Two Women at a Bar. Barcelona (1902). Oil on canvas, 31½ x 36″. (Leo and Gertrude Stein). Collection Walter P. Chrysler, Jr., New York. *Plate 27.*
"Collecting"… isn't something that I am interested in any more than that I am thrilled by big prices paid for works of art. I don't know what Chrysler paid for the two women's backs of Picasso that he bought from Gertrude but it was, I imagine, rather more than the forty dollars it set me back when I bought it.—Leo Stein, Journey into the Self, p. 268.

Woman with Bangs. Barcelona (1902). Oil on canvas, 23⅝ x 19¼″. (Leo and Gertrude Stein). The Baltimore Museum of Art, The Cone Collection.

Family Supper. Barcelona (1903). Watercolor and ink on paper, 12½ x 17″. (Leo and Gertrude Stein). Albright-Knox Art Gallery, Buffalo. *Plate 29.*

Seated Nude. (1903–4). Ink on paper, 15⅞ x 11¼″. (Leo and Gertrude Stein). Collection Mr. and Mrs. Georges E. Seligmann, New York.

"La belle qui passe." (1904). Ink on paper, 11 x 15″. Inscribed: "La belle qui passe." (Leo and Gertrude Stein). Collection Mr. and Mrs. Daniel Saidenberg, New York.

Boy with a Milk Can. Paris (1904). Gouache on cardboard, 24½ x 17¾″. (Leo and Gertrude Stein). Collection Mrs. Oveta Culp Hobby, Houston. *Plate 35.*

The Promenade. (1904). Ink on paper, 15¾ x 12″. (Leo and Gertrude Stein). Collection Mr. and Mrs. John D. Schiff, New York.

Seated Woman. (1904?). Ink on paper, 7⅞ x 5½″. (Leo and Gertrude Stein). Collection Mr. and Mrs. Richard K. Weil, St. Louis.

Study for *Young Acrobat on a Ball*. (1904). Ink on paper, 10 x 7″. (Leo and Gertrude Stein). Collection Sidney E. and Roberta Cohn, New York.

"Une tres belle danse barbare" (with letter to Leo Stein). (Drawing 1904; letter ca. 1905). Ink on paper, 11¼ x 15⅞″. Inscribed under drawing: "Une tres belle danse barbare." (Leo Stein). Collection Mr. and Mrs. Perry T. Rathbone, Cambridge, Massachusetts. *Page 27.*

Head of a Man (Mask). 1904–5. Bronze, 7¾″ high. (Leo and Gertrude Stein). The Baltimore Museum of Art, The Cone Collection. *Plate 38.*

Study for *The Actor* with Profiles of Fernande. Paris (Winter 1904/5). Pencil on paper, 19 x 12½″. (Leo and Gertrude Stein). Collection Nelson A. Rockefeller, New York.

Circus Family with Violinist. (1905). Ink and wash on paper, 7⅛ x 6½″. (Michael and Sarah Stein). The Baltimore Museum of Art, The Cone Collection.
This and the following three works are studies for *The Acrobat's Family with a Monkey.*

Monkey. (1905). Brush and pen and ink on paper, 7½ x 7¼″. (Michael and Sarah Stein). The Baltimore Museum of Art, promised bequest of Grace McCann Morley in memory of Sarah Stein.

Mother Caressing Child. (1905). Ink on paper, 8 x 5⅞″. (Michael and Sarah Stein). The Baltimore Museum of Art, The Cone Collection.

Profile Head of Woman. (1905). Ink and wash on paper, 7¼ x 5⅜″. (Michael and Sarah Stein). The Baltimore Museum of Art, The Cone Collection.

The Acrobat's Family with a Monkey. Paris (1905). Gouache, watercolor, pastel, and India ink on cardboard, 41 x 29½″. (Leo and Gertrude Stein). Konstmuseum, Göteborg, Sweden. *Plate 40.*

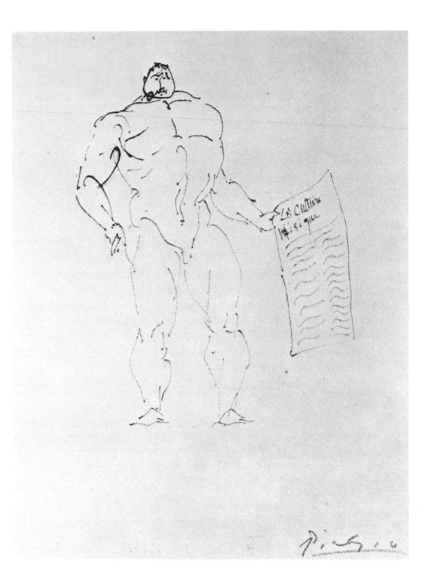

PICASSO. *Guillaume Apollinaire.* 1905.
Collection Lionel Prejger, Paris

Family of Harlequins. (1905). Ink on paper, 7⅝ x 7″. (Leo and Gertrude Stein). Collection Mr. and Mrs. Georges E. Seligmann, New York.

Four Nudes (verso: *Two Men Posing*). (1905). Ink on paper, 9½ x 12⅝″. (Leo and Gertrude Stein). Picard Collection.

Guillaume Apollinaire. Paris (1905). India ink on paper, 12¼ x 9″. (Leo and Gertrude Stein). Collection Lionel Prejger, Paris. *Page 165.*

It was before Gertrude Stein knew the rue Ravignan that Guillaume Apollinaire had his first paid job, he edited a little pamphlet about physical culture. And it was for this that Picasso made his wonderful caricatures, including one of Guillaume as an exemplar of what physical culture could do.–Gertrude Stein, Autobiography of Alice B. Toklas, p. 77.

Harlequin and Child. (1905). Ink on paper, 12¼ x 9½″. (Leo and Gertrude Stein). Collection Mr. and Mrs. Georges E. Seligmann, New York.

Head of a Boy. (1905). Gouache on composition board, 12¼ x 9½″. (Leo and Gertrude Stein). The Cleveland Museum of Art, bequest of Leonard C. Hanna, Jr. *Plate 39.*

Head of Woman in Profile. (1905). Drypoint, 11⅝ x 9¾″ (plate). (Leo and Gertrude Stein). The Museum of Modern Art, New York, Lillie P. Bliss Collection.

The Jester's Family. Paris (1905). Ink, colored pencils, and wash on paper, 6½ x 4⅞″. (Michael and Sarah Stein). Dumbarton Oaks Collection, Washington, D. C.

Seated Nude. Paris (1905). Oil on cardboard, mounted on panel, 41¾ x 30″. (Leo and Gertrude Stein). Musée National d'Art Moderne, Paris.

Sheet of Studies: Self-Portrait and Nudes. (1905). Ink on paper, 9½ x 12⅝″. (Leo and Gertrude Stein). Collection H. Arnold Steinberg, Montreal. *Plate 33.*

The Two Giants. Paris (1905). India ink on paper, 12⅝ x 8⅝″. (Leo and Gertrude Stein). Collection Jan Krugier, Geneva.

Two Harlequins. 1905. Pastel on paper, 27½ x 20½″. (Michael and Sarah Stein). Collection Mrs. Robert P. Hutchins, Manchester, Vermont.

Woman with a Fan. Paris, 1905. Oil on canvas, 39 x 32″. (Leo and Gertrude Stein). Collection the Honorable and Mrs. W. Averell Harriman, Washington, D. C. *Plate 37.*

Young Girl with a Basket of Flowers. Paris (Spring 1905). Oil on canvas, 61 x 26″. (Leo and Gertrude Stein). Collection Mr. and Mrs. David Rockefeller, New York. *Plate 32.*

After meeting Picasso I went again to Sagot's. Gertrude was with me this time and Sagot showed us a picture of a nude, almost naked little girl with a basket of red flowers. I liked the picture, but Gertrude hated it. A few days later I bought it. That day I came home late to dinner, and Gertrude was already eating. When I told her I had bought the picture she threw down her knife and fork and said, "Now you've spoiled my appetite. I hated that picture with feet like a monkey's." Some years after, when we were offered an absurd sum for the picture and I wanted to sell it—since for that money one could get much better things—Gertrude would not agree to sell, and I believe that she always kept it.–Leo Stein, Appreciation: Painting, Poetry and Prose, p. 173.

Gertrude Stein did not like the picture, she found something rather appalling in the drawing of the legs and feet, something that repelled and shocked her. She and her brother almost quarreled about this picture. He wanted it and she did not want it in the house. Sagot gathering a little of the discussion said, but that is alright if you do not like the legs and feet it is very easy to guillotine her and only take the head. No that would not do, everybody agreed, and nothing was decided.

Gertrude Stein and her brother continued to be very divided in this matter and they were very angry with each other. Finally it was agreed that since he, the brother, wanted it so badly they would buy it.... —Gertrude Stein, Autobiography of Alice B. Toklas, p. 52.

Study for *Boy Leading a Horse*. Paris (Winter 1905/6). Brush and sepia wash on paper, 19¼ x 12⅝". (Michael and Sarah Stein). The Baltimore Museum of Art, The Cone Collection.

Boy Leading a Horse. Paris (Winter 1905/6). Oil on canvas, 86½ x 51¼". (Leo and Gertrude Stein). Collection Mr. and Mrs. William S. Paley, New York. *Plate 36.*

Leo Stein. (ca. 1905–6). Ink on paper, 12½ x 9⅜". (Michael and Sarah Stein). Private collection. *Page 29.*

Leo Stein. (ca. 1905–6). Ink on paper, 6¾ x 4¼". (Leo and Gertrude Stein). Collection Mrs. Jerome B. Rocherolle, Stamford, Connecticut. *Page 28.*

Portrait of Gertrude Stein. Paris (1905–6). Oil on canvas, 39⅜ x 32". (Leo and Gertrude Stein). The Metropolitan Museum of Art, New York, bequest of Gertrude Stein, 1946. *Page 50.*

It was only a very short time after this that Picasso began the portrait of Gertrude Stein, now so widely known, but just how that came about is a little vague in everybody's mind. I have heard Picasso and Gertrude Stein talk about it often and they neither of them can remember. They can remember the first time that Picasso dined at the rue de Fleurus and they can remember the first time Gertrude Stein posed for her portrait at rue Ravignan but in between there is a blank. How it came about they do not know. Picasso had never had anybody pose for him since he was sixteen years old, he was then twenty-four and Gertrude Stein had never thought of having her portrait painted, and they do not either of them know how it came about. Anyway

it did and she posed to him for this portrait ninety times and a great deal happened during that time....

Spring was coming and the sittings were coming to an end. All of a sudden one day Picasso painted out the whole head. I can't see you any longer when I look, he said irritably. And so the picture was left like that.

Nobody remembers being particularly disappointed or particularly annoyed at this ending to the long series of posings. There was the spring independent and then Gertrude Stein and her brother were going to Italy as was at that time their habit. Pablo and Fernande were going to Spain.... Gertrude Stein, Autobiography of Alice B. Toklas, pp. 55, 64–65.

Immediately upon his return from Spain he painted in the head without having seen me again and he gave me the picture and I was and I still am satisfied with my portrait, for me, it is I, and it is the only reproduction of me which is always I, for me.—Gertrude Stein, Picasso, p. 8.

After a little while I murmured to Picasso that I liked his portrait of Gertrude Stein. Yes, he said, everybody says that she does not look like it but that does not make any difference, she will, he said.—Gertrude Stein, Autobiography of Alice B. Toklas, p. 14.

The Bath. (1906). Ink on paper, 11 x 16". (Leo and Gertrude Stein). The Art Museum, Princeton University, Princeton, New Jersey.

Boy on Horseback. Paris (1906). Ink on paper, 16 x 12¾". (Leo and Gertrude Stein). Collection Nelson A. Rockefeller, New York.

Chick, Blue Background. (1906). Woodcut, 5¼ x 4⅜". (Leo and Gertrude Stein). Collection Mr. and Mrs. John Hay Whitney, New York.
This and the following woodcut were made for a projected edition of Guillaume Apollinaire's *Le Bestiaire*.

Eagle, Red Background. (1906). Woodcut, 5⅝ x 4½". (Leo and Gertrude Stein). Collection Nelson A. Rockefeller, New York.

Head of a Woman. (1906). Pencil on paper, 9 x 6¾". (Leo and Gertrude Stein). Collection Dr. and Mrs. Frederick H. Low, New York.

Head of a Woman. (1906). Ink on paper, 12 x 9¼". (Leo and Gertrude Stein). Collection Mr. and Mrs. Georges E. Seligmann, New York.

Prodigal Son among Pigs (The Swineherd). (1906). Pencil and ink on paper, 8 x 7½". (Leo and Gertrude Stein). Collection Mr. and Mrs. Daniel Saidenberg, New York. *Plate 34. She was always fond of pigs, and because of this Picasso made and gave her some charming drawings of the prodigal son among the pigs.*—Gertrude Stein, Autobiography of Alice B. Toklas, pp. 108–109.

Seated Nude, Seen from Back. (1906). Ink on paper, 16⅛ x 11¾". (Leo and Gertrude Stein). Collection Mr. and Mrs. Richard K. Weil, St. Louis.

Standing Nude. (1906). Pencil on paper, 24⅞ x 18⅛". (Leo and Gertrude Stein). Museum of Art, Rhode Island School of Design, Providence, gift of Mrs. Murray S. Danforth.

Standing Nude. (1906). Pencil on paper, 12¼ x 9⅛". (Leo and Gertrude Stein). Collection Mr. and Mrs. Georges E. Seligmann, New York.

Study for *Woman Combing Her Hair.* (1906). Pencil on paper, 12 x 8¾". (Leo and Gertrude Stein). Collection Mr. and Mrs. Georges E. Seligmann, New York.

Portrait of Allan Stein. Paris (Spring 1906). Gouache on cardboard, 29⅛ x 23½". (Michael and Sarah Stein). The Baltimore Museum of Art, The Cone Collection. *Page 83.*

This portrait of their only child was painted as a birthday gift to Sarah Stein from her husband.

Portrait of Leo Stein. Paris (Spring 1906). Gouache on cardboard, 9¾ x 6¾". (Leo and Gertrude Stein). The Baltimore Museum of Art, The Cone Collection. *Page 12.*

Bust of Female Nude in Profile. Gosol (Summer 1906). Ink on paper, 10¾ x 7¼". (Michael and Sarah Stein). The Baltimore Museum of Art, The Cone Collection.

Standing Nude. Gosol (Summer 1906). Conté crayon on paper, 24½ x 18⅝". (Leo and Gertrude Stein). Collection Mr. and Mrs. Leigh B. Block, Chicago. *Plate 31.*
Study for *Standing Female Nude.*

Standing Female Nude. Gosol (Summer 1906). Oil on canvas, 60⅝ x 37¼". (Leo and Gertrude Stein). Collection Mr. and Mrs. William S. Paley, New York. *Plate 30.*

Study for *Two Youths.* Gosol (Summer 1906). Crayon on paper, 10⅛ x 6⅞". (Leo and Gertrude Stein). Collection Nelson A. Rockefeller, New York.

Letter to Leo Stein with Sketch of *The Peasants.* August 17, 1906. Ink on paper, 7 x 8⅞" (unfolded). (Leo Stein). Collection of American Literature, Beinecke Rare Book and Manuscript Library, Yale University, New Haven.

Head of a Young Man. Paris (Autumn 1906). Oil on canvas, 10¾ x 7¾". (Leo and Gertrude Stein). Collection André Meyer, New York.

Reclining Nude. Paris (Autumn 1906). Black crayon on paper, 18¾ x 24½". (Leo and Gertrude Stein). The Baltimore Museum of Art, The Cone Collection.

Studies for *Two Nudes.* Paris (Autumn 1906). Conté crayon on paper, 24 x 17¾". (Leo and Gertrude Stein). Museum of Fine Arts, Boston, Arthur Tracy Cabot Fund.

Two Nudes. Paris (Autumn 1906). Charcoal on paper,

24½ x 18″. (Leo and Gertrude Stein). The Museum of Fine Arts, Houston, gift of Governor and Mrs. W. P. Hobby.

Head in Profile. (1907). Conté crayon on paper, 5¾ x 7½″. (Leo and Gertrude Stein). Collection Mr. and Mrs. Jan Mitchell, New York.

Study for *Les Demoiselles d'Avignon* (*"Nez quart de Brie"*). (1907). Conté crayon on paper, 11⅞ x 9⅜″. (Leo and Gertrude Stein). Collection Mr. and Mrs. Georges E. Seligmann, New York.

Head. (1907). Gouache on paper, ca. 12 x 9″. (Michael and Sarah Stein) Collection Mr. and Mrs. Walter A. Haas, San Francisco.
Study for *Les Demoiselles d'Avignon.*

Head of Sailor. Paris (Spring 1907). Oil on canvas, 15¾ x 16⅝″. (Leo and Gertrude Stein). Collection Mr. and Mrs. David Rockefeller, New York.
Study for *Les Demoiselles d'Avignon.*

Head. Paris (Summer 1907). Oil on paper, 12¼ x 9½″. (Leo and Gertrude Stein). Private collection, New York.

Head. Paris (Summer 1907). Oil on paper, 12¼ x 9½″. (Leo and Gertrude Stein). Private collection, New York.

Head. Paris (Summer 1907). Tempera and watercolor on paper, mounted on panel, 12¼ x 9½″. (Leo and Gertrude Stein). Collection Nelson A. Rockefeller, New York.

Head (Head in Browns and Black). Paris (Summer 1907). Watercolor and gouache on paper, 12⅛ x 9⅜″. (Leo and Gertrude Stein). Collection Nelson A. Rockefeller, New York.

Study for *Nude with Drapery.* Paris (Summer 1907). Watercolor on paper, 12¼ x 9½″. (Leo and Gertrude Stein). The Baltimore Museum of Art, The Cone Collection.

Study for *Nude with Drapery.* Paris (Summer 1907). Oil

wash on paper, mounted on canvas, 12¾ x 9¾″. (Leo and Gertrude Stein). Collection Herbert and Nannette Rothschild.

Study for *Nude with Drapery.* Paris (Summer 1907). Oil on paper, 12¼ x 9½″. (Leo and Gertrude Stein). Collection Mr. and Mrs. Lionel Steinberg, Palm Springs, California.

Study for *Nude with Drapery.* Paris (Summer 1907). Gouache on paper, mounted on canvas, 12 x 9¼″. (Leo and Gertrude Stein). Collection Mrs. Maurice L. Stone, New York. *Plate 42.*

Study for *Nude with Drapery.* Paris (Summer 1907). Oil on canvas, 23⅞ x 18¼″. (Leo and Gertrude Stein). Collection Mr. and Mrs. John Hay Whitney, New York. *Plate 41.*

Nude with Drapery. Paris (Summer 1907). Oil on canvas, 59⅞ x 39¾″. (Leo and Gertrude Stein). The Hermitage, Leningrad. *Plate 43.*

Still Life with Lemon. Paris (Summer 1907). Gouache on paper, 12⅝ x 9½″. (Leo and Gertrude Stein). Collection Mr. and Mrs. David Rockefeller, New York.

Mask of a Woman. (1908). Bronze, 7½″ high. Collection Mr. and Mrs. Sampson R. Field, New York.
Gertrude and Leo Stein owned the original terracotta of this sculpture, now in the Musée National d'Art Moderne, Paris.

Still Life with Fruit and Glass. Paris (1908). Tempera on wood, 10⅝ x 8⅜″. (Leo and Gertrude Stein). Collection Mr. and Mrs. John Hay Whitney, New York. *Plate 45.*

Still Life with Glasses and Fruit. Paris (1908). Oil on cradled panel, 10⅝ x 8⅜″. (Leo and Gertrude Stein). Private collection, New York.

Still Life with Glasses and Fruit. Paris (1908). Oil on cradled panel, 10⅝ x 8¼″. (Leo and Gertrude Stein). Collection Nelson A. Rockefeller, New York. *Plate 44.*

Three Women. Paris (1908). Oil on canvas, 78¾ x 70⅛".
(Leo and Gertrude Stein). The Hermitage, Leningrad.
Plate 46.

*Against the wall was an enormous picture, a strange picture
of light and dark colours, that is all I can say, of a group, an
enormous group and next to it another in a sort of red brown,
of three women, square and posturing, all of it rather fright-
ening.*—Gertrude Stein, Autobiography of Alice B. Toklas,
p. 27.

Landscape, La Rue des Bois. (late Summer 1908). Oil on
canvas, 28¾ x 23⅝". (Leo and Gertrude Stein). Collection
Riccardo Jucker, Milan.

Landscape, La Rue des Bois. (late Summer 1908). Oil on
canvas, 28⅞ x 23¾". (Leo and Gertrude Stein). Collection
André Meyer, New York. *Plate 48.*

Landscape. Paris (Autumn 1908). Oil on canvas, 39⅝ x
32". (Leo and Gertrude Stein). Collection Mr. and Mrs.
David Rockefeller, New York.

Homage to Gertrude. (1909). Tempera on wood, 8¼ x
10¾". (Gertrude Stein). Private collection, New York.
*It was about this time too that he made for her the tiniest of
ceiling decorations on a tiny wooden panel and it was an
hommage à Gertrude with women and angels bringing fruits
and trumpeting. For years she had this tacked to the ceiling
over her bed. It was only after the war that it was put upon
the wall.*—Gertrude Stein, Autobiography of Alice B. Toklas,
p. 109.

Head of Woman. Paris (Spring 1909). Watercolor on paper,
19¾ x 13". (Leo and Gertrude Stein). Collection Jean
Masurel, Paris.

Vase, Gourd, and Fruit on a Table. Paris (Spring 1909). Oil
on canvas, 28½ x 23⅜". (Leo and Gertrude Stein). Collection Mr. and Mrs. John Hay Whitney, New York. *Plate 47.*

above PICASSO. *Homage to Gertrude.* 1909.
Private collection, New York

below PICASSO. *Houses on the Hill, Horta.* 1909.
Collection Nelson A. Rockefeller, New York

This is one of two still lifes lent by Leo Stein to the Armory Show in 1913.

Head of a Woman. Horta de Ebro (Summer 1909). Oil on canvas, 23⅞ x 20¼". (Leo and Gertrude Stein). The Art Institute of Chicago, The Joseph Winterbotham Collection.

Houses on the Hill, Horta. Horta de Ebro (Summer 1909). Oil on canvas, 25⅝ x 32". (Leo and Gertrude Stein). Collection Nelson A. Rockefeller, New York.

That summer they [Pablo and Fernande] went again to Spain and he came back with some spanish landscapes and one may say that these landscapes, two of them still at the rue de Fleurus and the other one in Moscow in the collection that Stchoukine founded and that is now national property, were the beginning of cubism.—Gertrude Stein, Autobiography of Alice B. Toklas, p. 109.

The Reservoir, Horta. Horta de Ebro (Summer 1909). Oil on canvas, 23¾ x 19¾". (Leo and Gertrude Stein). Collection Mr. and Mrs. David Rockefeller, New York. *Plate 49.*

The Architect's Table. Paris (Spring 1912). Oil on canvas, oval, 28⅝ x 23½". (Gertrude Stein). Collection Mr. and Mrs. William S. Paley, New York. *Plate 50.*

In the Spring of 1912, Gertrude Stein made her first independent purchase of a Picasso painting. Letters from Picasso and D.-H. Kahnweiler indicate that the price of 1,200 francs was difficult for her to pay. Picasso stuck to his price, and Kahnweiler arranged for payment to be made in two installments. Picasso referred to the picture casually as "votre nature morte (ma jolie)," but Kahnweiler identified the painting by its formal title, "La Table de l'Architecte."

The Little Glass. Paris (Spring 1912). Oil on canvas, 18¼ x 15⅛". (Gertrude Stein). Private collection, New York.

Still Life. Paris (Spring 1912). Oil and charcoal on canvas, 18¼ x 15¼". (Gertrude Stein). Collection Mr. and Mrs. John Hay Whitney, New York.

Study for *Violin*. Paris (Winter 1912). Crayon and charcoal on paper, 24⅝ x 18⅝". (Gertrude Stein). Marlborough Gallery, Inc., New York.

Violin. Paris (Winter 1912). Oil, sand, and charcoal on canvas, 21¾ x 17". (Gertrude Stein). Private collection, New York.

Study for *Guitar on a Table*. Paris (Winter 1912/13). Crayon on paper, 25 x 19⅛". (Gertrude Stein). Marlborough Gallery, Inc., New York. *Plate 53.*

Guitar on a Table. Paris (Winter 1912/13). Oil, sand, and charcoal on canvas, 24¼ x 20⅛". (Gertrude Stein). Collection Nelson A. Rockefeller, New York. *Plate 52.*

Man with a Guitar. Céret, Summer 1913. Oil and wax on canvas, 51¼ x 35". (Gertrude Stein). Collection André Meyer, New York. *Plate 55.*

Student with a Pipe. Paris (Winter 1913/14). Oil, charcoal, pasted paper, and sand on canvas, 28¾ x 23⅛". (Gertrude Stein). Collection Nelson A. Rockefeller, New York. *Plate 51.*

Woman with a Mandolin. Paris (Winter 1913/14). Oil, sand, and charcoal on canvas, 45½ x 18¾". (Gertrude Stein). Collection Mr. and Mrs. David Rockefeller, New York. *Plate 54.*

Cut Pear, Grapes, and Pipe. Paris (1914). Oil and sand on paper, 8 x 11½" (sight). (Gertrude Stein). Private collection.

Still Life with Ace of Clubs. Paris (1914). Oil, pencil, charcoal, and pasted paper on canvas, mounted on cradled panel, 17⅞ x 15". (Gertrude Stein). Collection Mr. and Mrs. John Hay Whitney, New York.

Still Life with Calling Card. 1914. Pencil and pasted papers on paper, 5½ x 8¼". (Gertrude Stein). Collection Mrs. Gilbert W. Chapman, New York. *Page 172.*

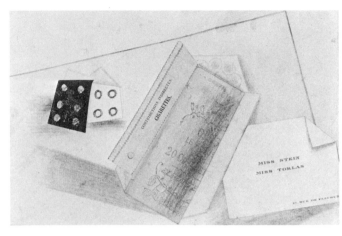

Still Life with Fruit, Glass, Knife, and Newspaper. 1914. Oil and sand on canvas, 13⅝ x 16½". (Gertrude Stein). Collection Mr. and Mrs. David Lloyd Kreeger, Washington, D.C. *Plate 56.*

Still Life with Bottle of Maraschino. Avignon (Summer 1914). Oil and charcoal on canvas, 15 x 18⅛". (Gertrude Stein). Collection Mr. and Mrs. John Hay Whitney, New York.

Apple. Paris, Winter 1914. Watercolor on paper, 5⅜ x 6⅞". Inscribed on back: "Souvenir pour Gertrude et Alice/Picasso/Noel 1914." (Gertrude Stein and Alice B. Toklas). Collection Mr. and Mrs. David Rockefeller, New York. *Pages 57-58.*

Guitar. Paris, Spring 1918. Watercolor on paper, 6¾ x 7½". Inscribed on back: "pour Gertrude Stein/son ami Picasso/Montrouge 26 avril 1918." (Gertrude Stein). Collection Mr. and Mrs. David Rockefeller, New York.

Picasso had just written to Gertrude Stein announcing his marriage to a jeune fille, a real young lady, and he had sent Gertrude Stein a wedding present of a lovely little painting and a photograph of a painting of his wife.

That lovely little painting he copied for me many years later on tapestry canvas and I embroidered it and that was the beginning of my tapestrying. I did not think it possible to ask him to draw me something to work but when I told Gertrude Stein she said, alright, I'll manage. And so one day when he was at the house she said, Pablo, Alice wants to make a tapestry of that little picture and I said I would trace it for her. He looked at her with kindly contempt, if it is done by anybody, he said, it will be done by me. Well, said Gertrude Stein, producing a piece of tapestry canvas, go to it, and he did.—Gertrude Stein, Autobiography of Alice B. Toklas, pp. 228–229.

Table with Guitar and Partition. Juan-les-Pins (1920).

above PICASSO. *Still Life with Calling Card.* 1914.
Collection Mrs. Gilbert W. Chapman, New York

below PICASSO. *Guitar.* 1918.
Collection Mr. and Mrs. David Rockefeller, New York

Gouache on paper, mounted on cardboard, 9⅝ x 7¼". (Gertrude Stein). Collection Mr. and Mrs. Gilbert W. Chapman, New York.

Calligraphic Still Life. April 2, 1922. Oil on canvas, 32⅛ x 39½". (Gertrude Stein). The Art Institute of Chicago, Ada Turnbull Hertle Fund. *Plate 57.*

Designs for needlepoint, executed by Alice B. Toklas as upholstery for two 18th-century chairs. (late 1920s). Collection of American Literature, Beinecke Rare Book and Manuscript Library, Yale University, New Haven.

HANS PURRMANN (?). 1880–1966

Still Life with Fruit. n.d. Oil on canvas, 18 x 24". (Michael and Sarah Stein). Collection Mr. and Mrs. Augustus Pollack, Carmel, California.

PIERRE-AUGUSTE RENOIR. 1841–1919

Bather. (1882–83). Oil on canvas, 21 x 16". (Leo and Gertrude Stein). Collection Mr. and Mrs. Algur H. Meadows, Dallas.

Brunette. (1890). Oil on canvas, 16¼ x 12¾". (Leo and Gertrude Stein). Collection Mr. and Mrs. Nelson R. Kandel, Baltimore. *Plate 22.*

The Reader. (ca. 1895). Oil on canvas, 8¼ x 6⅝". (Michael and Sarah Stein). The Baltimore Museum of Art, The Cone Collection.

The Two Bathers (from *L'Estampe Originale*). 1895. Etching, 10¼ x 9½". (Leo and Gertrude Stein). The Metropolitan Museum of Art, New York, Rogers Fund, 1922.

Landscape. n.d. Oil on canvas, 12⅝ x 13¾". (Leo and Gertrude Stein). The Baltimore Museum of Art, The Cone Collection.
Although the date of ca. 1917 is given in the 1934 catalogue of The Cone Collection, this seems to be the painting that appears in a 1904 photograph of the studio at the Rue de Fleurus.

FRANCIS ROSE. born 1909

Gertrude Stein. (1930–35?). Oil on canvas, 31½ x 25¼" (sight). (Gertrude Stein). Private collection.

PAVEL TCHELITCHEW. 1898–1957

Portrait of Gertrude Stein. 1930. Brush and India ink on paper, 16¾ x 11⅜". (Gertrude Stein). The Art Institute of Chicago, given in memory of Charles B. Goodspeed by Mrs. Gilbert W. Chapman.

FÉLIX ÉDOUARD VALLOTTON. 1865–1925

Gertrude Stein. (1907). Oil on canvas, 39½ x 32". (Leo and Gertrude Stein). The Baltimore Museum of Art, The Cone Collection.

MAHONRI YOUNG. 1877–1957

Portrait of Leo Stein. (ca. 1926). Terracotta, 12" high. (Leo Stein). Brigham Young University Art Collection, Provo, Utah.

Photocredits

All photographs have been supplied by the owners of the works reproduced, except in the following cases:
Baltimore Museum of Art, Cone Archives, pp. 88, 89, and photocopies for pp. 19, 23, 24, 37, 41, 90, 91, 92, 93, 94, 95; Edward Burns, New York, p. 61; Geoffrey Clements, New York, Pl. 37; Durand-Ruel, Paris, Pl. 19; Jean Gilbert, Paris, Pls. 43, 46; photocopy courtesy Mrs. Ellen B. Hirschland, Great Neck, N. Y., p. 82; Miss Nora Kaufman, Baltimore, p. 81; Knoedler Art Galleries, New York, Pl. 6; Lauros-Giraudon, Paris, p. 165; Courtesy of the Robert Lehman Collection, New York, Pl. 4; Pierre Matisse Gallery, New York, Pls. 1, 35; James Mathews, New York, pp. 69, 170, 172, Pls. 24, 25, 28, 30, 41, 45, 47, 48, 49, 50, 51, 52, 53, 55; photocopy courtesy The Museum of Modern Art, New York, p. 64; National Gallery of Art, Washington, D.C., Pl. 31; Perls Gallery, New York, Pl. 42; Eric Pollitzer, New York, p. 158; San Francisco Museum of Art, Pl. 7; John Schiff, New York, Pl. 34; Adolph Studly, Pennsburg, Pa., pp. 28, 29; Soichi Sunami, New York, pp. 12, 172, Pls. 8, 12, 13, 16, 36; Charles Uht, New York, p. 71, Pls. 32, 44, 54; Malcolm Varon, New York, Pl. 27; Mr. and Mrs. Christopher Wright, New York, pp. 15, 22, 39, 45, 53, 54; Yale University, Beinecke Rare Book and Manuscript Library, Collection of American Literature, pp. 17, 37, 74, 79.

Trustees of The Museum of Modern Art